THE THOROUGHBREDS

THE THOROUGHBREDS

Barbara J. Berry

The Bobbs-Merrill Company, Inc.
Indianapolis · New York

All rights reserved including the right of reproduction
in whole or in part in any form
Published by the Bobbs-Merrill Company, Inc.
Indianapolis   New York

ISBN 0-672-51829-5
Library of Congress catalog card number 73-16809
Designed by Paula Wiener
Manufactured in the United States of America

First printing

To Winnifred McCalpin Berry

Contents

The works of many fine scholars and authors have contributed greatly to the writing of this book. Anyone interested in more extensive information is urged to read these works for himself. They are listed in the bibliography on page 148.

I would also like to acknowledge the courtesy and helpfulness of the Jockey Club, the Tennessee Walking Horse Breeders and Exhibitors Association, and the United States Trotting Association.

Most valuable of all were the often taken-for-granted personnel of New York State's library interloan service. Bless them, and it.

Introduction

WHAT is the Thoroughbred?

It's the world's fastest racehorse, capable of running up to forty-five miles an hour carrying more than a hundred pounds on its back.

It's a bold, courageous jumper, undaunted by obstacles of appalling size, whether a solid wall six feet high or a complicated hedge-and-water jump ten feet across.

It's a beautiful horse, often an imposing sixteen or seventeen hands high and possessed of awesome grace and elegance.

But all of this only begins to describe the Thoroughbred, for its most outstanding quality, that which really sets it above the other horses of the world, is nearly indescribable. This quality has been called many things, such as the will to win, the inability to quit, and just plain "heart"; but none of these says it all.

Whatever this unique quality may be called, we can see it clearly when a Thoroughbred snaps a foreleg bone and refuses to be pulled up until the finish line has been crossed, or when a steeplechaser struggles riderless out of a thrashing pileup of horses and goes on to finish the course, taking all the formidable jumps alone. And now and then we can see it most clearly when a Thoroughbred is born with so much of that "something" that it quickly becomes a national hero, a superhorse among superhorses. Man o' War was our most recent such hero over fifty years ago.

What was it about Man o' War that so completely captured the heart, soul, and imagination of the entire country? That drew people with no other interest in horses or racing at all to the tracks in great crowds just to catch a glimpse of "Big Red"? If we can understand this, perhaps we can understand the basic quality of the Thoroughbred, perhaps even its very reason for being.

A man who watched Man o' War run felt something— something he'd remember all his life and tell his children and grandchildren about. The big red colt out there on the track that day, coming down the stretch "like a sheet of living flame," was much more than just another fast horse. He was a blending of speed, power, beauty, and "heart" that had never been seen before and would never be seen again. He was an arrogant, boisterous, swaggering personality, bouncing out onto the track full of the awareness of his immense superiority and fairly blazing with self-confidence. This, above all else, was what the man watching him felt, something that can best be described as true greatness. And for a moment the man could share this greatness. Such moments are rare, to be treasured.

It was for just such moments, in fact, that man struggled so hard to create the Thoroughbred, a racehorse of heroic proportions. He was actually fulfilling one of his most intense needs, the need to have a hero.

That he succeeded is proved every time a superhorse comes along. The very name "Man o' War" still means something to people even after all these years. Man o' War was not so much a racehorse as he was a hero.

While this may have been man's fundamental, underlying reason for the creation of the Thoroughbred, he probably didn't realize it. He thought he had a far more practical, down-to-earth reason. What could it have been? After all, the Englishman of the 1600s already had a perfectly good horse useful for every purpose. Why, then, did the English breeders devote themselves to the establishment of yet another, entirely new breed of horse?

The answer is quite simple. England had been a nation of horse racers from the time of the Romans at least, and by the 1600s this love of racing had become a raging passion—along with racing's inevitable companion, gambling. Enormous fortunes were wagered on the outcome of a single race, and nearly every wealthy aristocrat owned a racing stable. Obviously, the man who could breed the fastest horses could win the most races—and the most money.

Any underlying psychological motive aside, then, the horse we know today as the Thoroughbred was created for one purpose only: to run faster than any other kind of horse had ever run before. This it did, and with such spectacular results that this new breed, rightly called "a new creature on the earth," very soon set all England and then the entire world on its ear.

The next logical question after why is how. Once the Englishman decided he needed a faster horse, how did he accomplish this? This question isn't quite so easy to answer.

The story of the origins and development of the Thoroughbred starts a long time ago—several centuries—and this fact alone creates most of the difficulties. Take the matter of written records. Even as recently as the 1600s, when the new breed began to emerge as a distinct type, a man who could read and write simple sentences was considered rather well educated. Most people could not. Moreover, many of those who could have kept records didn't see any reason to. Therefore, such records are very scarce. What few we do find from this early period are likely to be incomplete, vague, and sometimes sheer inventions.

Much of our research is necessarily based, then, on a collection of rare, poorly kept records; the suspect word of excitable eyewitnesses; and the human memory, which of course is notable for its unreliability. A researcher soon begins to feel more like a detective, and history becomes more like a mystery story!

At first we find this hard to believe. Nowadays we're used to everything being meticulously documented, and nothing could be more exact and complete than the way modern Thoroughbreds are kept track of. Because of the Jockey Club, the Thoroughbred Racing Association, and all the state racing controls, there is very little chance for any fiddling of records. Thoroughbreds today are photographed, tattooed, and "fingerprinted" within an inch of their lives.

One or two hundred years ago, however, there was no certain way even to tell that a horse really *was* the horse somebody claimed it was. To complicate matters, before the breed became official, with its own registry, many horses were known by two or more different names, while others had no names at all—and a horse that achieved any fame was likely to have hundreds of other horses named after it. Naturally, this incredible casualness about names led to all sorts of confusion. It also led to some perfectly delightful entries in the very old pedigrees, too, like "Lady d'Arcy's

Pet Mare" and "Sister to Old Country Wench." But while these names are fun to find, they often add little to accurate identification.

Added to the dearth of records and the confusion about names, we find romantic but improbable legends; "traditions" with no discoverable basis in fact; theories, arguments, and opinions; and outright lies.

People were probably no more or less dishonest then than they are now. But with so few records, so much general vagueness, and no official registry, the opportunities for sharp dealing were a great deal more numerous. Added to the honest mistakes and the poor memories, then, we have the considerable problem of the invented pedigree. And there's no doubt whatever that many pedigrees were nothing but imaginative fiction. One rather stunning example of this common practice can be seen when research turns up the "fact" that one famous sire and one famous mare between them apparently produced fifty or sixty foals!

All is not nearly so hopeless as it seems, however. Fortunately for us, many fine scholars have devoted years of their lives to the serious study of the Thoroughbred, and their writings are extremely helpful.

A great deal of the mystery does remain unsolved. One is left wondering if perhaps some of the "legends" might not have been true, after all; and the scholars' opinions differ widely about many details. But the Thoroughbred's story is a fascinating one, fraught with hairbreadth escapes, incredible adventures, and noble deeds fit to break the heart. It's a story well worth investigating.

THE THOROUGHBREDS

1

The Arabian Theory

THE STORY of the Thoroughbred, or of any modern breed of horse, actually begins in ancient times. And so do the arguments over the true origins of the Thoroughbred's ancestors.

One argument, that which enjoys the biggest following, is that the Thoroughbred breed is mainly the result of the crossing of "native English mares" with imported "Arabian" stallions. Quotation marks are used here because as we'll see in a moment both these terms are at least questionable. Since these two types of horses were indisputably the root stock of the Thoroughbred, it's rather important that we try to find out exactly what they were. Besides, it's an interesting puzzle. Let's start with the "Arabians."

In our role of detective we first discover that the word "Arabian" was used very loosely by the Englishman of the 1600s; in fact, there was considerable confusion then as to what he meant by it. If we here and now define an Arabian as a horse bred and raised in Arabia, or whose immediate ancestors were (which seems reasonable enough), we further find that in all likelihood most of those horses called Arabians during those centuries were not Arabians at all, but Barbs and Turks.

Judging from fossils, conditions of climate and forage, and ancient writings, it seems most probable that the original wild ancestor of all three types first evolved and proliferated not in Arabia but farther north in the regions of Mesopotamia and what was then ancient Armenia, and that eventually, as man discovered, tamed, and developed the wild horse, he began to move outward from this cradle of civilization, taking his horses with him. This original ancestor of the horse gradually took on characteristics suitable to its new environment (as did man, for that matter). Thus was established, for instance, the Barb of northern coastal Africa, a somewhat different type from the Turk, which remained closer to home.

The Bedouin tribes of Arabia claim to have been raising fine horses for as many as four thousand years, and while most of Arabia is now arid desert, recent geological discoveries show that it has not always been so. Beneath the sand there have been found limestone rock and soil such as are found in Kentucky and Tennessee, which produce our famous bluegrass. Geologists now tell us that Arabia was once, many centuries ago, a "land of forests and pastures." So there well may be a basis for the Bedouin claim.

The fact remains, however, that by the year 1500 Arabia had long been a desert region, separated from the thriving horse-raising and horse-trading activities to the north by vast stretches of nearly uncrossable sand and heat. Moreover, by 1500, while horses were abundant and of high quality in those northern areas (such as Turkey, Armenia,

Syria, Morocco), in Arabia they were relatively scarce animals. The Bedouins were by then camel raisers, not horse raisers, and had been for a long time.

Aleppo, in Syria, was a famous horse market, and it was there that the Englishman of the 1600s bought many of his "Arabians". As John H. Wallace, one of the best students of horse history, pointed out in 1897, Aleppo had a huge supply of good horses which were available just to the north in Armenia and were continually being traded along the already well established route to North Africa. Why, then, Mr. Wallace wondered, would a Bedouin cross that enormous, terrible desert to sell what was to him a quite rare and very valuable animal in the glutted horse market of Aleppo? Mr. Wallace's blunt answer to his own question was that most, if not all, of the "Arabians" purchased at Aleppo were a case of "English 'tenderfeet' among Syrian horsethieves." These purchases, he claimed, would more accurately be described as Turks and, some of them, Barbs, notwithstanding the long, involved romantic histories that came with them, telling of heroic deeds on the Arabian desert and Arabian pedigrees going back to "a time man remembereth not."

Whether Mr. Wallace was right or not, it is certainly true that nothing whatever was really known for sure about the history or pedigree of any of these "Oriental" imports prior to their purchase by Englishmen.

"Oriental", the term given generally to all three types, may be the best one, since it's the vaguest. By the 1600s England was in the throes of a great Oriental craze that had begun long before with the returning crusaders. Anything "Oriental" was high style. "The Orient" meant those lands discussed above, to the east and south of the Mediterranean. Ladies gave exotic parties, dressed as they imagined Oriental ladies dressed, and sometimes even kept little black boys, whom they called blackamoors, dressed up in Moorish costumes.

It's not surprising, then, considering how important a part of life horses were in those days, that Oriental horses would become part of the general rage. And these imports were beautiful horses, most of them, unlike the typical native English stock. They were more lightly built, with the delicate legs, high-arching, graceful necks, and small, dainty heads that English horses usually lacked.

And now we get to the sore point of the argument. If the Oriental horse—be it Barb, Turk, or Arabian—*was* crossed with the native English horse to produce, in time, the Thoroughbred (and that much seems certain), what were the Orientals' actual contributions to the new breed?

Avid Arabianists like Lady Wentworth claimed that the Arabian contributed everything to the Thoroughbred—speed, size, stamina, and beauty—and that the English horse was in fact worthless to the new breed, the mares merely serving as sort of incubators for the Arabian stallions' offspring. Others don't go quite that far, but many do give most of the credit to the imports, maybe just from long-standing habit.

The facts would indicate otherwise. The native English horses of those times, to begin with, were far from worthless. They had been bred and developed for centuries for various purposes, and there were many useful types among them by 1600.

The first horses to set foot in the British Isles were probably brought there by those famous traders, the Phoenicians, dealing for tin several centuries before Christ. Later, about fifty years before Christ, the Romans "discovered" Britain and brought in more horses. Considering the locations of Phoenicia (near the Mideastern horse markets) and Rome, it's pretty safe to say that these first English horses were mostly of the Turk variety. During the following centuries many more horses were imported—from Flanders, France, Spain, and Morocco—and what was by 1600 called the "native English horse" was really a composite of many different types from all over.

There was the Great Horse, for instance, developed during the Middle Ages, which could carry up to four hundred pounds of knight in armor without its knees buckling. When the invention of firearms made armor obsolete (and the Saracens' little Barbs and Turks ran circles around the Great Horses during the Crusades), these huge, ponderous animals were put to work at heavy farm labor—a less glamorous occupation but far safer than being a charger. Then there were the ponies that developed on the rough moors and islands off Great Britain, the miserable climate and poor forage turning them into even smaller and tougher beasts than their small, tough ancestors.

Between these two extremes were the saddle and carriage stock of England, and it was from this stock that the racehorse, with a boost from the Orientals, eventually developed.

From Ireland came the Irish Hobbie, a marvelous little horse that was the favorite riding horse of England for at least a hundred years, until it suddenly lost favor about 1600. It was a fast horse, one that could pace or gallop at a good clip. Its pacing tendencies really endeared it to English riders, though: a gliding motion without the hard jolting of the trot.

There was also a well-established type, bred by a group of English monks, called both "the pacing Galloway" and "the racing Galloway," a fast galloper that figures prominently in pre-Thoroughbred bloodlines.

The cob, England's all-time favorite, was a common, rather homely little horse; in fact its name, "cob," refers to its roughness and coarseness. But it was a name given affectionately. Its smallish size, calm disposition, easy gaits, and stamina made it an ideal mount for man, woman, or child. There are still plenty of cobs in England.

And in Norfolk County there was a distinct type being developed, a somewhat larger pacing and trotting horse. This Norfolk horse, with its high, stylish trot and bearing, was already well on its way to being England's most fashionable carriage horse and would one day form the foundation for at least two new breeds, the Hackney and the Standardbred. As we'll see, the Norfolk horse also had an important influence on the beginnings of the Thoroughbred.

This, then, was the "worthless" native stock that contributed nothing to the Thoroughbred. Nothing?

How about speed? Hobbies and Galloways, especially, had been bred for speed for generations! For proof as to how successfully, we turn to England's most respected horseman of the time, Mr. Gervase Markham, who wrote in 1606:

For swifteness what nation has brought forth the horse which excelled the English? When the best Barbaries that ever were in their prime, I saw them overcome by a black Hobbie, of Salisbury, and yet that black Hobbie was overcome by a horse called Valentine, which Valentine neither in hunting nor in running was ever equalled, yet was a plain English horse, both by syre and dam.

This was no isolated instance, either, for the records show that the imported Orientals were so slow that they were finally, by regulation, given weight (allowed to carry less weight in races than the native horses, which of course gave them an advantage). Even so, they were nearly always beaten by the "plain English horses." So much for the side of the family from which the Thoroughbred acquired its great speed.

As for stamina, the English horse was not "worthless" in that respect either. The Duke of Newcastle, Master of the Horse and England's foremost horseman about that time, had this opinion of the Oriental's "superior stamina":

They talk they will ride fourscore miles in a day and never draw the bridle. When I was young I could have bought a nag for ten pounds that would have done as much *very easily.*

One man's opinion? Again we refer to the regular practice of giving weight to the Orientals. In the four-mile heat races of the day, stamina was perhaps even more important than speed, and again, even with an advantage, the Oriental couldn't beat the English horse. And once a test was made on the Orientals' home ground, the Egyptian desert. The best Arabs that the pasha's stable could produce were raced over eight miles of this desert—a pretty good test of stamina—against a middling good Irish Thorough-bred mare. The mare won easily.

What about size, then? The average imported stallion was about fourteen hands high, no larger than most and smaller than many English horses of that period. Considering that most modern Thoroughbreds stand at least sixteen hands high and that most modern Arabians are still around the fourteen- to fifteen-hand mark, the claim that the Arabian was solely responsible for the Thoroughbred's rather sudden increase in size sounds a bit hollow.

That only leaves us with one contribution: beauty. The English horses, while fast, sturdy, and eminently useful, as a rule were not particularly noted for beauty, so here the Oriental can perhaps finally make a claim stick. The Barbs, the Turks, and the occasional honest-to-goodness Arabian (which didn't look much different from one another) *were* beautiful horses, as we've said, and no doubt the cross did add stylishness to the new breed.

But the real contribution of the Oriental was its fresh blood. There comes a time in the history of any breed or type of horse when an outcross—the introduction of a completely different bloodline—is desirable. This the Orientals—purchased, captured in battle, or stolen—provided. Their fiery desert blood seems to have been just what the already developing English racehorse needed to "re-invigorate the native character."

What resulted was almost a mutant, a new kind of horse unlike either of its parents and superior to both. It was called the English running horse, the English blood horse, and finally the Thoroughbred.

Hundreds of fine mares contributed to the new breed. But owing to the "tail-male line" method of reckoning pedigrees, where only the direct line from sire to sire is given much notice, and the then-common practice of not bothering to name mares, the stallions got most of the credit. (It would be a very long time before geneticists could convince horse breeders that a mare furnishes exactly the same number of chromosomes to her offspring as does the stallion.)

Of the many good stallions that were involved, three were so outstandingly influential that they were soon designated as *the* three basic foundation stallions among the Orientals. Every Thoroughbred has descended from one or more of those three: the Byerly Turk, the Darley "Arabian," and the Godolphin "Arabian."

2

The Byerly, the Darley,
and the Godolphin

THERE'S a great deal of superstition and magic attached to the number three. "Good things come in threes" is one popular saying, and in the case of the early history of the Thoroughbred this seems to have been true. We must always keep in mind, though, that these three Oriental sires were not the *only* ones in England, by a long shot. One historian fixes the earliest Oriental importations (after those very first Phoenician and Roman ones) in the ninth century, and by his count there were at least 174 such stallions in England by the 1700s.

But of all those imports, the male lines of only "the big three" still exist, as far as anyone knows, and they are the direct ancestors of the second big three—Herod, Matchem, and Eclipse.

The first of the three immortal Orientals to arrive in England, in 1689, was the Byerly Turk. The first volume of the Stud Book says, "The Byerly Turk was Captain Byerly's charger in Ireland, in King William's Wars." It was said that Captain Byerly acquired this stallion by capturing him during the Battle of Buda, and the horse has been described as "a magnificent black charger." While the Stud Book calls him a Turk, there are those who claim he was really a pure-blooded Arabian. Actually, of course, we have no way of knowing either what his bloodlines were or any of his history before his capture. He is recorded, however, as being the great-great-grandsire of Herod, and if nothing else about the stallion is true, this would be enough to make him tremendously important.

Even less is known about the second of the three, called the Darley Arabian. He was imported from Aleppo in 1703 or 1704 by Thomas Darley (some say he traded a gun for the horse) and thought to be about four years old at the time. Whether he was an Arabian or not is very uncertain, but like so many others, he is always *called* one. Other than that, about all we can say about this stallion is that according to reports he was a "handsome" bay, marked with white socks behind and a blazed face.

Like the Byerly Turk, the Darley's greatest claim to fame came from his progeny rather than his own accomplishments. The Darley was never raced, and if the Byerly was, he certainly made no great splash. One of the Darley's sons was *Bulle Rock, the first Thoroughbred stallion to be imported to the American colonies. Another son, Flying Childers (mistakenly but popularly known as "Mile-a-Minute Childers"), was the fastest horse of his time and through *his* son Blaze founded both the Standardbred and Hackney breeds.

It was Flying Childers' full brother, Bartlett's Childers,

---

* An asterisk before a horse's name simply means "imported."

though, that figured so prominently in what would be the Thoroughbred line. Bartlett's Childers was never raced because he was a bleeder, so we'll never know if he was as fast as his famous brother. But he surely carried the genes necessary for speed, and his great-grandson Eclipse was spectacular proof of that fact.

And now we come to the Godolphin Arabian, also known (a confusion we can expect by now) as the Godolphin Barb. This legendary stallion's name and story are well known to anyone who has ever had even a passing interest in horses, and entire books have been written about him. If you're thinking that—at last!—we have come to a horse about which everything is really known, though, I'm afraid you're in for a disappointment. Even the Godolphin's postimportation history has been greatly romanticized. The legend of the Godolphin is so entertaining that to omit it because it can't be proved would be to omit the best part of the story. But as we go along, let's try to separate fact from fantasy as much as possible.

Fantasy (probably): The horse was foaled in Arabia about 1724 in a wealthy prince's stable. He was named Zenada and often called Scham, which means "the chief." Early in life, probably as a yearling or a two-year-old, he was sent, along with several other prized horses, by the prince (or, as another version has it, the emperor of Morocco) as a special gift to the king of France. Accompanying the colt was his beloved mute groom and his mascot, a cat. Because of their fiery temperaments, small size, or poor condition after the long voyage by ship, these gift horses were not only "looked in the mouth" but unwanted, and were soon sold or given away. Zenada eventually found himself in the hands of a poor Frenchman, pulling a water cart (or a wood cart) around Paris. His imperious disposition led him to fight his owner's cruelty, resulting in even more cruelty, while the mute groom and the cat skulked around Paris keeping a fearful eye on their friend but powerless to help him. Finally, when the underfed, weakened, and beaten-up horse went down in his shafts one day, collapsed on the street and was being brutally whipped, he was rescued by a kind Quaker Englishman who somehow "sensed his greatness" and bought him on the spot. Immediately, the groom and the cat came out of hiding to join their hero, and all three were sent off to England.

Fact (probably): At least some, if not most, of this story was made up of whole cloth, as were the fantastic histories of so many of the Oriental stallions. It does seem pretty well authenticated that the kindly Quaker, Mr. Coke, did find the horse in dire straits in Paris and did buy him—either because he "sensed his greatness," or because he simply took the quickest and surest way of easing the poor animal's suffering. Therefore, Zenada apparently *was* in Paris. But how and when he got there and where he actually came from will always be a mystery. Our favorite doubting Thomas, Mr. Wallace, thought that while the Godolphin was a great horse, he was most likely a native French horse of Spanish Barb ancestry, judging from written descriptions, the more accurate portraits of him, and from the fact that France and Spain had many such horses at that time.

There is also a considerable authority for believing that the stallion, on reaching England, was accompanied by a Moorish groom. Whether this groom actually had been with the stallion since its foaling, as is sometimes claimed, or merely happened on the rescue scene in Paris and saw a good chance to get to England is debatable. One thing that always puzzles me is how often the groom is quoted—it was he, apparently, who unfolded the long tale of glory and woe—yet he is usually said to have been mute. There are other ways than by speech to get ideas across, of course, but a name like Zenada? In sign language? Nevertheless, most versions and records seem to agree that there *was* a mysterious groom who loved the stallion dearly and never parted from him.

Fact (probably): Once in England, the stallion became the property of the owner of a London coffeehouse. For some reason (some say the horse tried to savage—attack— him or his stable men), he gave or sold the stallion to Lord Godolphin, who had a racing and breeding stable at Gog Magog.

Fantasy (probably): Among other horses, Lord Godolphin had a fine, highly thought of stallion named Hobgoblin, a grandson of the Darley. He also owned a beautiful, well-bred mare named Roxanna. Soon after Zenada's arrival at the farm, the stallion spied Roxanna, instantly fell in love with her, and for her favors attacked Hobgoblin, her rightful "husband," and—some go so far as to say—killed him. Then he mated with the fair Roxanna, and she produced Lath, who was instantly recognized as a superior animal. Where- upon the Oriental stallion's true worth as a sire was realized; he was proudly named the Godolphin Arabian (or Barb) and was set for life.

Fact (more probably): The new stallion and his groom were hardly more than tolerated at Gog Magog. The horse was small, a plain dark bay or brown color and not really beautiful. The most authoritative and reasonable-sounding accounts have it that he was used as a "teaser" for the snobbish Hobgoblin. If a mare is not ready to be bred and a stallion is offered to her prematurely, she is quite apt to resent him and show it by lashing out at him. Rather than risk injuring a valuable stallion, then, a teaser is often offered first—another stallion, usually one not worth much.

If the mare seems agreeable, then the valuable stallion is used. It was this inglorious but useful job that the Oriental stallion likely would have been given at first.

There are several versions of what happened next, including the fight-to-the-death. It seems improbable that the Oriental groom, no matter how determined to prove his charge's potential, would deliberately allow him to damage his master's most-prized stallion, let alone kill it—or even, if he was a horseman worth his salt, allow two stallions to get close to each other. The best sources seem to agree, though, that Roxanna passed the "tease test" but then haughtily refused even to entertain the notion of mating with Hobgoblin. This is not quite so romantic as it sounds. Mares will do things like that for reasons known only to themselves. On the other hand, she seemed receptive to the little Oriental. So, probably not to waste a good mare for the season, Lord Godolphin allowed the new stallion the honor.

At any rate, about eleven months later, in 1732, Roxanna produced a foal, and there seems to be no argument over its paternity. The colt was so slab-sided he was named Lath, but he couldn't have been too ill thought of, since Roxanna was a year later rebred to the new stallion. Lath's full brother, foaled in 1734, was named Cade.

Perhaps little of any of these versions is true. Perhaps what transpired was actually very prosaic and unremarkable. But in any case, when Lath got to the racecourses in 1737 and "proved what he could do," followed in 1738 by Cade and another great son, Regulus, the Godolphin's reputation as a sire of racehorses was established. These three sons were all entered in different races in one day at Newmarket that year; all three of them won; and the Godolphin Arabian was ceremoniously presented to the admiring crowd as their proud sire.

These three winners were followed by many more, and

most proved to be good breeding stock, too. Lath never sired anything special, but Cade was a superb sire, "getting high-class racers from all sorts and conditions of mares." Then, in 1748, sired by Cade out of "A Sister to Miss Partner," along came Matchem, and the Godolphin's place in equine history was secure for all time. He lived out his life in comfort at Gog Magog, the most sought-after sire in England, dying in 1753. His tombstone may still be seen near the stable.

Fact or fantasy? Does it matter? Not really. What matters is that the bloodlines of these three Orientals (and some "plain English mares") in time produced the first three stallions that could be called Thoroughbreds.

3

Matchem, Herod, and Eclipse

THE SECOND trinity, known as the "pillars of the Stud Book," came along from two to four (horse) generations later. To make the relationships between the two sets of three a little clearer, the tail-male lines run this way:

The Godolphin sired Cade, who sired Matchem.

The Byerly Turk sired Jigg, who sired Partner, who sired Tartar, who sired Herod.

The Darley sired Bartlett's Childers, who sired Squirt, who sired Marske, who sired Eclipse.

Or, with importation and foaling dates where known:

Darley Arabian	*Byerly Turk*	*Godolphin Arabian*
(imported about 1704)	(imported 1689)	(imported 1730)
Bartlett's Childers	Jigg	Cade, 1734
Squirt, 1732	Partner, 1718	Matchem, 1748
Marske, 1750	Tartar, 1743	
Eclipse, 1764	Herod, 1758	

These are only the direct sire lines, or "tail-male lines." It should be kept in mind that the complete pedigrees of the second three would each show several crosses of all three originals in the female lines. For instance, while Eclipse is called a Darley horse because of the direct sire line, his pedigree contains at least two crosses of Godolphin blood. Eclipse's own dam was a granddaughter of the Godolphin through her sire, Regulus.

But also notice the importation and foaling dates, as this will help to understand the relationships in time, too. Obviously, the Godolphin made the quickest impact on English blood stock, Matchem being foaled only eighteen years after the Godolphin's arrival and only two generations later. But by that time (1730) the Darley and the Byerly had already done their work. The Thoroughbred line was already well on its way, and the Godolphin, a relative latecomer, had mares with Darley and Byerly blood to help him make his reputation.

The puzzle, in short, was beginning to reach completion, and the picture—a new breed of horse—was already taking a definite shape.

Matchem, foaled in 1748, was the first of the second trinity. He was a bay horse, bred by Mr. John Hoomes of Carlisle. (Or Mr. Charles Hoomes, depending on what source you're reading, such was the state of records then.) Matchem's sire, of course, was Cade, the second son of the Godolphin and Roxanna, and his dam was "A Sister to Miss Partner," a daughter of the great racehorse Partner. His breeding, therefore, could be expected to produce something rather special, and it did. Some call Matchem a mutant, since at slightly over fifteen hands he was nearly a hand taller than either of his parents and far superior to them in speed. A dull bay in color, with only a few white hairs on coronet and face, he was considered plain, but he was noted for his extremely powerful shoulders and high withers. He was, in fact, a prototype of the coming new breed and may be said to be the first real Thoroughbred.

Like most racehorses of his time, Matchem wasn't asked to race until he was five years old. Since the races often consisted of three heats of four miles each, it took a mature, well-developed horse to compete in them. His racing career was not spectacular, as Eclipse's would be later on, but he won more than his share of those grueling races, enough to attract considerable attention. And such was the careful training and handling of racehorses in those days, and the bred-in stamina of the horses, that Matchem raced for ten years, retiring at the age of fifteen on a happy note, having just won an important race in which he beat a horse with the wonderful name of Sweetlips. At first his stud fee was only five guineas, but by 1775 it had risen to fifty, a pretty good indication of the quality of his foals. He was twenty-seven years old by then, but he produced nineteen foals that year. He died in 1781, thirty-three years old. It's interesting to contemplate that when Matchem was foaled, the American colonies hadn't yet thought seriously of rebelling, but by the time he died, the United States of America was well under way.

Herod, the second "pillar of the Stud Book," was foaled exactly ten years after Matchem, in 1758. He was bred by that serious student of pedigrees, the Duke of Cumberland. Herod was a deliberate attempt by the duke to produce "the perfect racehorse."

He had watched Matchem and felt that Matchem was definitely a step in the right direction, but was perhaps a bit too fine—too "Oriental." So he bred the good stallion Tartar (a great-grandson of the Byerly Turk) to his unraced mare Cypron, who carried Darley blood in her veins. The result, in Herod, was very close to what the duke wanted, a large bay horse standing 15.3 hands—or 16.1, again depending. It may be well to mention here that a great deal of the confusion over the exact height of horses is not due so much to careless measuring and recording as to the fact that through history the hand itself has been variously measured at three, four, and five inches. Now, of course, it is standardized at four inches.

In any case, it seems certain that King Herod, as he was originally named by the duke, was a good deal taller than his parents and the average racehorse of his day. He was described as being "mighty of shoulder and rump, with loop-arching neck." Another prototype, approaching the size and powerful ranginess of the modern Thoroughbred. He, too, began racing at five years old and did so creditably but not remarkably, retiring to the stud in 1770, while old Matchem was still going strong. For a long time after Herod died, his line was the most important of the three. But eventually it was overcome by the fantastic success of the other two and virtually "eclipsed" by a horse deserving a chapter of his own.

4

Eclipse

ECLIPSE has been called the first truly great racehorse, and that statement, sweeping as it is, would be impossible to dispute. He was also, in all probability, the most influential breeding animal that ever lived. Today approximately 90 per cent of Thoroughbreds descend from this fabulous stallion. And his glory was not confined to his breeding success; unlike his Oriental ancestors, he was something of a racehorse, too. Nowadays, we have the Horse of the Year. Eclipse did better than that. It's quite possible that he was the fastest racehorse of his entire century.

This triumph of "scientific breeding," at a time when much horse breeding was haphazard at best, was also an accomplishment of the Duke of Cumberland. The duke himself rates a few words here since by producing two of the three "pillars" he may have been the most important single breeder the Thoroughbred line has ever had.

Descriptions of the duke present a dismally unattractive picture. According to them, he was grossly obese, about 300 pounds, limped badly from an old war wound complicated by gout, had only one good eye, and was possessed of a brilliant red nose owing to his great fondness for the bottle. He apparently divided his time between his beloved decanters and his equally beloved stables, for one lady wrote in her diary that he "smelt like a drunken horse!"

Unattractive though he may have been, the Duke of Cumberland was a man to whom we should all be grateful. His obsession with the perfect racehorse led to Eclipse.

Eclipse's strange story began in 1764 when he was foaled under a bad omen (an eclipse of the sun, which terrified many in those days) on All Fools' Day, April 1. In fact, it seemed to the duke, who had hoped for so much, that the new colt was a horrid April Fools' joke.

The duke had studied pedigrees for years, trying to choose exactly the right mate for his favorite mare, Spiletta. Beside being called "the most beautiful mare in the world," Spiletta, a granddaughter of the already legendary Godolphin, and possessing Darley blood as well, had superb bloodlines. She looked like a pure Arabian, although she was not. So anxious was the duke to find just the right stallion for this prized mare that she was fourteen years old before he finally made up his mind. The duke's friends, if he had any, must have been appalled when he announced the big decision, for he had chosen the stallion Marske.

Marske seemed an unlikely choice, to put it most kindly. Putting all his faith in pedigrees, the duke had chosen a runty, sway-backed stallion the color of mud to mate with the gorgeous Spiletta. Not only that, Marske's sire, named Squirt because he was even runtier than Marske, had been destined for dog meat until a sympathetic groom saved him. But the duke wasn't so blind or so insane as he seemed.

Marske was an eyesore, but he carried a generous dollop of Darley blood, and the duke's long hours over the pedigrees had convinced him that this beauty-and-the-beast combination would give him what he longed for: a racehorse finer than Herod, stronger than Matchem, and faster than either.

What he saw that black All Fools' Day threw him into bitter, raging disappointment. At the lovely Spiletta's side was the *ugliest* colt he—or maybe anyone—had ever seen. A muddy chestnut with a single comical white stocking all the way to one hock and a too-wide blaze on its crude, huge head, it was truly a sight to dispirit anybody. As an eyesore, it outshone even its sire. The duke was shattered. He ordered the monstrosity fed to the hounds.

Fortunately, he soon relented. It was, after all, Spiletta's colt. And so Eclipse lived—and grew. By the time he was a yearling, he was nearly as tall as his dam and noticeably taller than other yearlings. He did not, however, grow any less ugly, and it was soon found that he had a disposition to match. The grooms all feared his terrible temper, and when he was turned loose with the other young horses, he proved to dislike them as much as he did people. To keep the other colts from being savaged, Eclipse had to be put in solitary confinement.

Watching this colt grow, the duke must have felt that fate had done its worst; as it turned out, fate had still one more cruel trick in store for the duke.

On October 31, 1765, Allhallows Eve, the duke suddenly died. Eclipse, the despised, ugly caricature of a colt, was only one and a half years old, and so the Duke of Cumberland died still believing that his great experiment had been a miserable failure. Had he been allowed to live only a few more years!

The duke's tragic fate seemed to switch to Eclipse

himself. Seldom if ever has a horse of such vital importance to a breed led such a hair-raising life.

At his untimely death, the duke's blood stock was sold at auction. Herod, a proven racehorse, brought a good price from Sir John Moore, another aristocratic horse breeder. But Eclipse—with his ridiculously long neck, barrel, and legs, his huge, homely head, his oddly high hips that made him look as if he were standing with his front feet in a hole, and his all too obvious disposition—was sold to a portly little squire, a London meat dealer, named William Wildman. The price he paid, seventy or eighty guineas, was high enough to make it clear that he was not buying meat on the hoof, but the jokes about steaks and chops flew.

Mr. Wildman, however, ignored them. He had long yearned for real acceptance by the aristocracy, and he was out to gain this by beating them at their own game—horse racing. He had a small stable near Epsom Downs and a few not very successful racehorses. All he needed, he was sure, was just "one good horse" to gain admittance to the closed circle of the racing gentry.

Why he thought Eclipse might be that horse, no one can say, but choose him he did. He was to regret this choice many times.

For with all his other faults it soon became apparent that Eclipse was also untrainable. As time went on, the big colt remained so vicious that all attempts to break him ended in disaster. And the world came close, for the second time, to losing the "most valuable breeding animal that ever lived." Mr. Wildman was constantly advised to geld the savage stallion. Only then, he was told, would there be any chance of subduing him. What good, after all, was a racehorse that couldn't be ridden?

Fortunately, Mr. Wildman planned to breed horses someday, and he valued Eclipse's bloodlines highly. But as one roughrider after another tried and failed to break him, and time to race drew ever nearer, he must have been severely tempted to resort to the gelding knife, if not, indeed, to the butcher's block.

Then, just in time, along came George Elton, and another strange episode in Eclipse's life began. It seems that Elton was more than just another roughrider. Fresh out of jail, he may have been a highwayman (a common enough profession in those days), and it seems fairly certain that he was a poacher. He was just the "tough guy" to break the tough Eclipse.

He not only broke him, he proceeded to ride him night and day. By day, as was the custom then, he rode Eclipse over hill and dale, strengthening him for the long, exhausting races to come. And by night, it seems, Elton used the fantastically speedy Eclipse as a "getaway horse" on his forages into other people's woodlands.

Once again, it seems a miracle that Eclipse survived. The hard use alone would have broken down an ordinary horse. And in those days poaching was a very serious crime. Gamekeepers, with full official approval, shot first and didn't bother to ask questions. But somehow Eclipse survived both the brutal training and the gamekeepers' shotguns.

In fact, Eclipse was a big, strong horse, and Elton's unorthodox training methods only served to strengthen him more. His legs, although considered absurdly long, had always been powerful—one of his few good points—and under Elton's regime his muscles turned to steel. Also, he was what was called a "powerful breather"—an extraordinary lung capacity caused him to breathe noticeably even when at rest—and Elton's hard working hours increased this ability. Later, four-mile heats and all, Eclipse never became the least bit winded; he was a horse "that could run forever."

Eclipse's other great strength, his undefeatable spirit, didn't suffer under Elton's attentions either. His willful, bullheaded, savage cussedness never wilted. Elton could ride the horse, but he admitted he could never really control him. He didn't mind losing a few arguments with the big horse, though. After all, whether Elton realized it yet or not, he was riding the fastest horse of the century, which must have been pretty convenient some nights.

George Elton's good fortune came to an end when Eclipse reached his full growth in 1769. He was a five-year-old, and it was time for him to race. Mr. Wildman moved his big, long-geared horse the few miles to Epsom Downs.

There Mr. Wildman, who all this time had retained his faith in Eclipse, resisting all the temptations and advice to geld or butcher the funny-looking, evil-tempered horse, ran into another seemingly insurmountable problem.

Eclipse, thanks to George Elton's courage and perseverance, was "broke"—he would, if he felt like it, tolerate a rider on his back. But even at five years old he wasn't really trained, and everyone whom poor Mr. Wildman consulted was of the firm opinion that the horse would never be trained enough to race. Eclipse might run, all right, but as people kept pointing out to Mr. Wildman, there was more than that to racing. No horse, they told him, could possibly run all out for four long miles. If it tried, it would surely collapse long before the finish line. It had to be controllable so that the jockey could hold it back a bit at times, down to a reasonable speed, saving enough strength and wind for that crucial last half-mile or so.

For a time that spring it seemed as though Mr. Wildman, so close to his goal, might be stymied. In the first place, none of the jockeys wanted to ride Eclipse. Who'd want to ride a horse that everyone laughed at, that looked as if it were standing with its front feet in a hole? Besides, everyone knew that only a short-coupled, short-backed horse had any speed, and this chestnut monster of Mr. Wildman's towered over the other horses and was ridiculously rangy. Even had they been willing, riding Eclipse looked like an impossibility. Eclipse still fought being saddled, bridled, and ridden. He kicked, bit, reared, bucked, and in general won no friends among the potential riders. On top of everything else, he had a weird habit of suddenly and unexpectedly "exploding" for no reason anyone else could see. This did not endear him to the jockeys, either, and soon Eclipse became known at the Downs as "bull-headed," "savage-tempered," "unmanageable," and not altogether sane.

Then once again fate stepped in at the last possible moment and produced exactly the right jockey to ride Eclipse—and one who, moreover, dared to try it. His name was John Oakley, and he possessed the two necessary qualities for riding a horse like Eclipse: He was not afraid of him, and he was intelligent enough to realize that there was only one possible way to ride an uncontrollable but very fast horse, and that one way was to try to steer him—keep him on the course—but otherwise just let him run.

At this point, a merry rogue named Captain O'Kelly entered Eclipse's life. O'Kelly was a low-born Irishman who, through cleverness, daring, and sometimes unethical finagling, had charmed his way into England's upper crust. It was Captain O'Kelly, for instance, who came up with the idea of hiring a group of people to do nothing but keep an eye, and a stopwatch, on horses' prerace workouts in order to furnish bettors with this valuable information. The idea succeeded so well that "O'Kelly's Gang" (the world's first professional touts) soon had competition from other gangs, all getting up early in the mornings to watch the workouts.

So in a way O'Kelly was responsible for Mr. Wildman's next problem. Wildman knew his horse was fast, but he preferred that nobody else should know it, at least not until he could safely get his bets down at profitably long odds. Should any of the touts find out how speedy Eclipse was before his first race, the information would be passed along, and the odds would plummet. Mr. Wildman knew that if Eclipse raced the way he *could* race this first time out, he would never again get such an opportunity to clean up. He'd have to do it, if at all, before Eclipse's speed became common knowledge.

This wasn't Mr. Wildman's only remaining problem. Eclipse was entered in a race to be run on May 3. Since it would be his very first race, it was vital that he get a chance beforehand to try out the course, preferably with a trained, reliable racehorse to accompany him as a good example. Unfortunately, Mr. Wildman did not own another racehorse that was nearly fast enough even to keep Eclipse in sight. And if he asked any of the gentry to lend him one of their horses, his secret would soon be all over London. What to do?

Thus it was that the extremely respectable Mr. Wildman teamed up with one of the wildest con men of all time, Captain O'Kelly. O'Kelly was nothing if not shrewd, and it appears that he guessed at the well-hidden greatness of Eclipse. As soon as he saw the horse there at Epsom Downs, he began to cozy up to Mr. Wildman, and when the meat dealer eventually confided his problems, he offered not only to furnish one of his own horses as a work mate but to keep it a secret. He, too, of course, planned to make money hand over fist on the prerace wagering if all went as hoped.

Consequently, O'Kelly invited all the touts to come see the new horse Eclipse work out. But he invited them to come an hour after the workout was scheduled. It was almost still dark out that morning when Eclipse and O'Kelly's horse, a winning racehorse, were sneaked out to the course. The workout went fine, and the touts all arrived "on time," which is to say, an hour too late to see anything. It was a great idea that O'Kelly had had, but like a lot of great ideas, it didn't quite work. The touts were not only disappointed, they were suspicious. And the secret leaked.

A talkative old woman who lived near the edge of the racecourse had seen the whole thing, or as much as could be seen in the near darkness. For a suitable payment she told one of the touts that yes, she had seen two horses out very early that morning. And yes, one had had a white leg. Then, growing more excited, she told the fascinated tout that the horse with the white leg had run right away from the other horse, apparently with no effort at all. "A monstrous runner," she called the white-legged horse!

As a result, Wildman and O'Kelly had to hustle to get their bets down at favorable odds, and it's a good thing they did, because as soon as word of the remarkable workout got around, the odds went to one-to-four, very short for an untried horse.

Eclipse's debut at Epsom Downs on May 3, 1769, was a harbinger of things to come. It was, in fact, a real humdinger. Running for the prize of fifty guineas were five good horses: Eclipse, Gower, Chance, Social, and Plume. The distance was the usual four miles, in three heats, or twelve miles altogether.

In the first heat Eclipse more or less behaved himself, and John Oakley brought him home an easy winner. O'Kelly was so encouraged by this that he made the most famous bet in racing history for the second heat. With the odds zooming to one-to-twenty, O'Kelly bet all comers that he could write down on a piece of paper the placing of every single horse in the race! This seemed so impossible that he had plenty of takers. He wrote down his predictions and gave them to someone to be read to the public when the heat was over.

In the second heat Eclipse really began to get the hang of horse racing. Oakley just let him go, and the result was that they crossed the finish line well over a furlong (an eighth of a mile) in front of all the rest of the horses.

In those days there was a rule that any horse winning by more than 200 yards (a furlong is 220 yards) was recorded as having "distanced the field." When that happened, which was almost never, the rest of the horses simply weren't placed at all. They just awarded first place to the winner.

So that's how the clever O'Kelly won his famous bet, for when his prediction was made public, it read, "Eclipse first, the rest nowhere."

This only added to the considerable stir already caused by Eclipse's astonishing speed. After all, he had just won his very first race in two heats, both times crossing the finish line not only far ahead of the rest but—even more unbelievable—at a strangely wallowing, spraddle-legged but unhurried hand gallop! The horse that was built all wrong was making the horses that were built right look like a herd of crippled pigs. Obviously something was amiss. It didn't take long, especially with O'Kelly involved, for suspicions to flare up, and when Eclipse's powerful breathing was noticed, a demand went up to see if the horse was doped.

It was a reasonable demand, as most certainly Captain O'Kelly was not above tampering with a horse if the situation seemed to require it. So Eclipse was duly examined, and of course he was found innocent. (The last thing that wild, ungovernable stallion needed was something to pep him up.)

Well, now, O'Kelly knew he had to get his hands on

Eclipse, and he was just the man to know how to go about it. He offered to help Mr. Wildman some more, this time with the ever-present problem of Eclipse's vile disposition.

O'Kelly's stable master was another Irishman named Sullivan. Sullivan was also well known, but in a different way. It was said that he could turn the most savage horse into a pussycat in just a few minutes. How, nobody was quite certain, as Sullivan wasn't telling. Some guessed that he hypnotized them; others insisted that he worked his miraculous "cures" by breathing into the horses' nostrils, although what good that would have done remains a mystery. At any rate, and however he did it, the fact was that there were plenty of formerly mean horses around that Sullivan had transformed into regular pets.

So when O'Kelly generously offered the services of his horse tamer to the already grateful Mr. Wildman, the result was an even more grateful squire. Sullivan "did his thing," whatever it was, with Eclipse. Whether it worked or not is hard to say now. Eclipse went on to race, and apparently he never actually killed anybody, but on the other hand he continued to be famous for being a bad actor. The important thing to O'Kelly was that now he and Mr. Wildman were bosom buddies.

When Eclipse moved on to Ascot and won his second race even more easily than the first, O'Kelly took advantage of Mr. Wildman's gratitude and bought a half-interest in the horse that the squire probably would never have given up otherwise. By the end of that season, with Eclipse still winning everything he entered without once extending himself, O'Kelly bought him outright, having paid altogether about 1,750 guineas for the horse. That wasn't a bad price, really, considering how small the race prizes were, and anyway, Mr. Wildman really didn't need Eclipse anymore. He was well known by this time and firmly entrenched in high society, thanks to his having owned such a fabulous racehorse.

O'Kelly could no longer make such profitable bets as he had for Eclipse's first race, of course. Bettors were few and far between who would wager against the superhorse. O'Kelly would have to wait until Eclipse retired to the stud to make any more real money on him.

By the opening of Eclipse's second racing season in 1770 there was already a scarcity of owners willing to race a horse against him. Even the year before, in fact, at three different times Eclipse's competition had all been withdrawn as soon as he was entered, and he'd been forced simply to gallop over the course all by himself to collect the prize, a "walkover."

Then, at Newmarket in the spring of 1770, Eclipse finally—for the first and last time—met a horse that was good enough to challenge him.

That horse was Bucephalus, oddly enough Eclipse's "uncle," although they were both six years old. It must have surprised Eclipse, who was used to romping along far ahead of the others, to find the smaller Bucephalus sticking to him like a burr. For the very first time Eclipse had to exert himself, and the first three and a half miles were covered at record-breaking speed as Bucephalus, contrary to all probabilities, displayed tremendous courage by pushing himself to the very limit of his powers for that entire heartbreaking distance. Heartbreaking it was, too, because with only half a mile left to go Eclipse decided he'd better hustle himself. He put on an effortless burst of speed then that the brave but exhausted little Bucephalus simply could not match. He tried valiantly, but collapsed on the course, broken in leg, wind, and spirit. He was never able to race again.

After that race it was "no contest." A few other horses were put up against Eclipse in hopes of perhaps being able to stay close enough to get a second or a third, but Eclipse often distanced the field and cheated them out of even that much, and three more times that season he ran his own private little walkovers.

Thus it was that after three grueling years of training, Eclipse raced only two years. But those two years were so astounding that they turned England's horse-breeding theories upside down. By the time Eclipse had finished two years of whipping the daylights out of anything that dared to cross his path, the horse breeders were thoroughly converted. The same men who had laughed themselves silly at Eclipse's ugliness were now frantically searching the countryside for long-necked, long-backed mares that looked like they were standing on a downhill slope!

Captain O'Kelly would probably have liked to race Eclipse another year or two, but all the circumstances were against it. No competition, therefore no betting action; and the handicappers had taken to putting 168 pounds on the horse, an unheard-of weight even in those sturdy days. So Eclipse was retired at the ripe old age of six years.

But problems still dogged the greatest horse of the century. From all over England mare owners were beating a path to O'Kelly's door, fat breeding fees in hand, but he had a horse that, in spite of Sullivan's ministrations, apparently loathed all other living things. In spite of their eagerness to get foals sired by the great Eclipse, few breeders would feel too pleased about having their valuable mares savaged or even killed. Eclipse was still a "rogue elephant," almost as unruly and evil as he'd ever been.

With so much at stake there was only one thing to do: hunt up a worthless mare and see what happened.

For one last time fate intervened in a seemingly hopeless situation and redeemed it. It would have been a catastrophe if after all his narrow escapes Eclipse had proved to be unbreedable. But O'Kelly's latest desperate gamble was successful. Eclipse, the savage brute, took one look at the homely old farm mare he was first introduced to and was instantly smitten. No mere human had ever really tamed him, but the first mare he met did. Once romance entered the picture, Eclipse settled down to a life of contented, slippers-and-pipe domesticity.

For nineteen years Eclipse sired racehorses, and such racehorses! Crop after crop of them went to the tracks and most of them won. By the time he died in 1789, at the respectable old age of twenty-five, there was no doubt in anyone's mind as to his real worth, and he was such a prepotent sire that he firmly stamped all his sons and daughters—and even their sons and daughters, for generations to come—with his unmistakable mark of greatness.

Eclipse's story is a story of ifs. If the kind groom hadn't rescued Squirt, Eclipse's grandsire. If the Duke of Cumberland hadn't chosen the unlikely Marske. If Eclipse had been "fed to the hounds," or gelded, or butchered. If Elton hadn't been out of jail at the moment. The list goes on and on.

But Eclipse was allowed to live, and he was finally broken, and he did race. And because of Eclipse, the duke's "failure," a magnificent new breed came into the world. We call it the Thoroughbred. The Duke of Cumberland would have called it "the perfect racehorse."

5

The English Racing Scene

With Herod, Matchem, and Eclipse we are now well into the 1700s. A lot had been happening to English horse racing during the previous hundred years or so, and the scene was set for the progeny of these three sires to sweep the field.

English monarchs from very early times had encouraged racing by their own avid interest in it. Henry VIII, reigning 1509–47, was a big fan of horse racing, and he made many laws designed to improve the horse stock in size, number, and quality. One set of laws was especially important. In those days it was common for livestock to roam at large, wandering and breeding as the mood struck them. So Henry VIII decreed that only stallions over a certain minimum height (fifteen hands in Norfolk, fourteen hands in other counties) could be turned loose; the penalties for disobeying these laws were severe. He also ordered that every archbishop and duke must raise at least seven stallions fourteen hands high or over and that every man whose wife wore a velvet hat must keep a horse or suffer a fine. He also established more royal studs, breeding centers where fine stallions were available to good mares.

Other monarchs continued the interest, donating prizes (such as King's Plates) for the races; some of them even rode their own racehorses. King Charles II, reigning 1625–85, was one such royal jockey, so enamored of racing that ambassadors and other important visitors often had to seek him out at the Newmarket racecourse, which he made England's second capital by his constant presence there.

Queen Anne, reigning 1702–14, was one of the most enthusiastic of all the British monarchs, loving both hunting and racing. She imported several Orientals and had her royal park, Ascot, turned into what became and has remained England's most fashionable racecourse.

Many annual classic races were inaugurated during this period. In the United States "the Derby" means the Kentucky Derby to most of us. But everywhere else in the world it means the first and greatest one, the English Derby. And it's a matter of the sheerest luck that we do not talk about "the Bunbury" instead.

Charles Bunbury and young Lord Derby were two of many wealthy, high-minded aristocrats who did much to improve the racing scene in England. One spring morning in 1780 Lord Derby and some of his guests attended a race at Newmarket for three-year-olds. It was the first running of what was to become the great classic race of England, and as yet it had been given no title. In a friendly fashion Lord Derby and Mr. Bunbury tossed a coin, the winner to claim the new race as his namesake. Lord Derby won, obviously. Mr. Bunbury's horse, however, got even for him by winning the first Derby. It was a horse named Diomed, a stallion that would years later be so important to the American Thoroughbred.

Newmarket had been a famous racecourse since about 1600. But in 1752 it became more important than ever when a couple of noblemen leased some land there from a horse dealer and had the Jockey Club Coffee Room built on it.

Jockey Club seems an odd name to us now for a collection of dukes, lords, and earls. But the name is derived from the fact that in racing's early times there were few professional jockeys. The aristocrats often rode their own entries; that was part of the sport of it. "Horses were horses" in those days, too, and while they were small by modern standards, they could carry a normal-sized man four miles at full tilt and then come back and do it again in the second and third heats. The idea of gaining more speed by putting a lightweight rider up came later. So, many of these first jockeys of the Jockey Club had actually earned the title by riding in races.

Horse racing, with its gambling, prizes, and opportunities for trickery, has always attracted the wrong as well as the right kind of people. When, about 1750, the respectable gentry heard about some blatant irregularities being committed at Newmarket that year, they met at the Red Lion Inn to decide what action to take. Horse racing, after all, was the Sport of Kings and wealthy aristocrats, and so it was deemed fit that they should control it. This they did, so well and so honorably that the group soon became the recognized authority over all racing in England. Their first official regulation in 1758 concerned the weight of riders.

The Jockey Club now also oversees the publication of the Racing Calendar and the General Stud Book, licenses jockeys, and in general still runs horse racing in England and keeps it honest.

Had those honorable men not seen and accepted this great responsibility, English horse racing would soon have deteriorated to the point where the public would have lost both faith and interest in it. Nobody but the fixer wants to bet on a fixed race. However, interest grew all the time.

During this century or so, from about 1700 to 1800, English racing gradually took on a new look. It was becoming more sophisticated. The horses were getting taller and faster, and by the end of the century the dream of the English horse breeder had come true: The Thoroughbred had been fully developed into a distinct type.

In 1791 the introduction to the first volume of the Stud Book was printed by Robert Weatherby at the direction of the Jockey Club, and regardless of what Mr. Wallace and others thought about Weatherby's choices and histories, this was the first attempt at the official listing of the foundation stock. That it was based more on traditions, faulty memories, and fantasies than on accurate knowledge doesn't detract from its real importance as a milestone in the history of the breed. It is rather fun to recall this shaky beginning, when we find later on how snobbish the British could get about American Thoroughbreds' early bloodlines. (To this day, for instance, many English breeders insist that Man o' War was not really a Thoroughbred.)

There were other milestones and important changes during this period. Charles Bunbury, as just one example, was very influential in getting England's racecourses gradually to give up those brutal four-mile heat races and begin to run younger horses at shorter distances in single heats. The first Derby, in 1780, was a mile and a half for three-year-olds—something unimaginable a half-century before.

In the latter half of the 1700s England's five great classics were all inaugurated: The St. Leger for three-year-olds of both sexes in 1776; the Epsom Oaks for three-year-old fillies in 1779 (the name came from Lord Derby's second residence, The Oaks, a converted brewery where he lived alone to escape a shrewish wife); the Two Thousand Guineas for three-year-old colts in 1809; and the One Thousand Guineas for three-year-old fillies in 1814. These races have never lost their prestige and are all still world-famous some hundred and seventy years later.

But perhaps one of the most important of the gradual changes taking place during the 1700s concerned the class of people who participated, or at least watched. Racing had begun as an occasional casual set-to at a country market, progressed to the Sport of Kings, and queens, and now once again began to include the ordinary citizen. This greatly affected racing's constant shadow, gambling.

Before, betting was accomplished among the gentry in private, in their homes or the elite coffeehouses: huge fortunes were wagered between and among gentlemen. But the common spectator, once he was allowed to watch the races, also caught the gambling fever. While he had no huge fortune to risk, he had his pennies, and (with O'Kelly's help) the professions of tout and bookmaker blossomed.

It might be interesting to note here that the word "tout" evidently is a distortion of "toot." To attract the attention of the crowd to their professional services, touts and bookmakers would let go occasional blasts on tin horns. Thus also our expression, "tinhorn gambler."

At first the bookmakers were discouraged, sometimes by law, but they proved impossible to stamp out and soon became accepted, as they still are in England, as legitimate, respectable, and, anyway, inevitable businessmen. And, to the general public at least, gambling became one of the most important aspects of racing.

On occasion this aspect has given racing a black eye, but on the other hand, it has kept the general public interested and is probably more responsible than anything else for the fact that the breeding, raising, and racing of Thoroughbreds is a multimillion-dollar industry today. (Some of the horses, for that matter, are multimillion-dollar horses.)

A reminder: These English racehorses came predominantly from English stock, stock that had been bred for generations for speed. Any Oriental crosses may have helped simply by introducing new blood but probably did little to improve the speed of the English racehorse directly. The English running horse did not get its speed from, as Mr. Wallace put it, "some supposed 'Arabian' cross away back ten generations, that never ran in his life." English horse breeders may not have had the benefit of modern theories of biology and genetics, but they were certainly well aware of the fundamental method of breeding fast horses: to breed winners to winners. This is exactly what they did; and, at about the same time, so did their American cousins in the colonies, using the developing English racehorse for their root stock.

6

Colonial Horse Racing

An EARLY ancestor of the horse existed in North America untold eons ago, but for unknown reasons it vanished, leaving only fossils to arouse our curiosity. The first North American horses of modern times were imported from Europe.

After his first trip in 1492 Columbus returned and this time brought a few horses with him, which he left behind in the West Indies. These were followed by the Spaniards' horses in the 1500s. So by the time the English colonists first arrived in Virginia in 1607, building some cabins and calling them Jamestown, there were already quite a few horses on the continent: in Mexico, in what are now our Southwestern states, and around the Caribbean. These were horses of Spanish Barb descent, such as were being imported into England about this same time. But between Jamestown and the nearest horses lay hundreds of miles of nearly impenetrable wilderness, so they were of no help to the colonists at all.

And Jamestown needed its horses. Every cabin built, every little scrap of land cleared for growing food meant long hours of heartbreaking hand labor, cutting down, sawing, and moving trees and stumps, and a horse could do the work of several men. There must have been some horses in the very first fleet of three ships in 1607, because later the settlers reported home that the following winter had brought a disastrous famine and that they had been forced to eat all their livestock, "and our horses and mares they had eaten with the first." The next record we find about horses is dated 1620 when the colony's sponsors sent them twenty more mares, "beautiful and full of courage." This and subsequent batches fared much better than the first. It wasn't long, in fact, before "the woods were full of horses," literally, and a favorite pastime of youngsters was trying to catch them.

These were horses of that good old native English stock: thirteen to fourteen hands high, of mixed Irish, Scottish, and English blood, and prone to the pacing gait, which was already beginning to lose favor in England as the Englishman learned to post to the trot.

At first the Jamestowners had neither spare time nor strength to spend on racing, and no place to race. Every bit of land that wasn't taken up by cabins or essential food crops was thick with huge trees. But soon the old English love of horse racing prevailed. The streets between the cabins were short, narrow, and full of holes, but they were cleared, at least. The first horse racing in the colonies was what would now be called "street drags." Street drags are illegal now because obviously they are a menace to all concerned, and the same was true back then. It got so bad that a lady couldn't cross the street with any safety. So nearly every early settlement's first laws dealt with street racing. That this didn't stop the dangerous sport is evident from the court records, but at least laws made it illegal and somewhat pacified the ladies.

The Virginians' next step, when their races were no longer welcome on the streets, was to move out into the woods. With terrific labor, "straight and narrow paths" were cut through the wilderness. They were only a quarter of a mile long, which was a long distance considering the effort involved in clearing them. "Quarter pathing," a brand-new kind of horse racing, was thereby invented. While England was still running its four-mile heat races, the colonists, doing the best they could under the conditions, were running these short, fast races. There was only room for two horses at a time on the narrow paths, and the quick, sturdy little horses were soon taught to get off to a fast start and do a blazing turn of speed for the quarter-mile. In other words, they became sprinters.

These quarter races got pretty wild sometimes. Horses jumped the gun and were forced into the trees, so strict judging was required at both ends of the path to keep the race honest. So high did sentiment run among the spectators and bettors, in fact, that disputes were often of a violent nature, and the judges were picked both for their honesty and their ability to defend themselves and their decisions with their fists.

But times changed in Virginia, too. The Virginians began to make profits from their tobacco crops. Newer settlers were aristocrats escaping from Cromwell's regime. Slave labor was introduced. A whole new way of life—that of the "Southern gentleman"—approached rapidly. Racing, and the raising of racehorses, became a prime concern of the gentry. Quarter pathing went out of style as more land was cleared; the settlers could afford to buy English racehorses, and the new aristocracy sneered at the little "quarter pathers." The native stock, combined with the Chicasaw horse of the Indians (a Barb descendant), moved west and south. Later on, helped tremendously by a stocky Thoroughbred import named *Janus, it would become the famous Quarter Horse.

The Virginians, South Carolinians, Marylanders, and New Yorkers, meanwhile, used much of their new wealth to bring over Thoroughbreds. The Thoroughbred wasn't fully and officially established until around 1800, of course, but these imports, called "breds," "bloods," or simply racehorses, were of the same stock that was evolving into the new breed in England. There were hundreds of such imports, especially in the South, before the Revolutionary War. Some were genuine, and some no doubt had forged pedigrees, but the effect was to speed up the old Irish-Scottish-English mix and eliminate in the racing stock the tendency to pace. The South soon became the undisputed breeding center of blood stock and remained so until the Civil War.

The North, however, was far from horseless. New Englanders also received horse stock from the mother country, the same kind of horses that the South started out with. But the people and the conditions were different up North, and the horses they developed became different, too. The two main reasons for this divergence were roads and religion.

The North built more roads sooner than the South did. While the Southerner was faced with mud much of the year and had to ride because wheeled vehicles were unusable, the Northerner needed road horses for his buggies and wagons. Road horses, of course, meant trotters and pacers, exactly what England was sending over.

Furthermore, the Southerner's religion tended to be Church of England, which was a rather sporting religion, not at all opposed to horse racing. The New Englander's religion was sterner. Horse racing was considered a vice, and for a long time it wasn't even tolerated. Still, the Northerners were Englishmen, too, and the native love of a good horse race couldn't be kept down altogether. And so a wonderful rationalization resulted. "Horse racing" was interpreted to mean running races. Pacing and trotting didn't count. Thus deacons and preachers touched up their trotters and pacers for a quick brush on the road, without any injury whatever to their consciences. These brushes were very common, often set up in advance, but they were not "official," not recorded, so we know little about them. As the decades passed, however, New England's trotters and pacers got larger and faster, doubtless not by accident. The Narragansett Pacer, developed in Rhode Island, became especially well known.

The New Yorkers, though, got there first with the most in regard to racetracks. England took over "Newe Amsterdam" from the Dutch during the reign of King Charles II, the monarch who made Newmarket his home away from home. And practically the first official act of the first English governor of New York, in 1665, was to order a racetrack built on the level plain of Long Island. To make even more points with King Charles, the governor named the track New Market. It was a success from the start, and in following years many more tracks were built in and around New York City and on Long Island. One Long Island track, the Union Course, which opened in 1821, would one day become the site of the "North-South" races, the most thrilling and devastating sporting events in American history.

Meanwhile, during the 1700s, racecourses were flourishing, on and off, in all the colonies. "On and off" because as times and sentiments changed back and forth in each colony, horse racing would be first popular, then abolished, then brought back again. Generally speaking, though, the annual or semiannual race meets at Long Island, Annapolis (where a certain Mr. George Washington was a regular visitor), and the other tracks were the highlights of the social seasons. At Annapolis, particularly, the meets were attended by the "best" people and accompanied by a round of parties and elegant balls. If one wanted to see the most famous men of the period all at one place at one time, the extremely fashionable racetracks were where one would find them.

Therefore, racehorses were naturally being bred. As in England, they were developed from what was at hand or could be imported. This meant the little pacer-trotter, by now America's native horse, and, as the colonists could afford them, the bred, starting with *Bulle Rock, brought to Virginia in 1730. Newspaper ads of the time represent this stallion as being of "the best English blood," sired by the Darley out of a Byerly mare. We do not know how successful this horse was as a sire, or even what happened to him, as no further record of him has been found.

During the next forty years many such English racehorses were imported into the colonies, and the new breed, the Thoroughbred, developed almost apace with its English counterpart.

Then revolution began to appear inevitable, and the colonists prepared themselves for the coming conflict. The great struggle that followed had a tremendous effect on racing, as it did on everything else. The most immediate effect on racing was to halt it completely. Patriotic Americans abandoned it for more serious pursuits before, during, and for a short time after the war. Also, while the British officers were here, they confiscated and took back to England most of the good racehorses. Others were killed in the line of duty. A crucial message could only be sent as fast as a horse could carry it, and these fast horses were highly valued for their importance to communication.

But the most injurious effect of the Revolution on the development of the Thoroughbred in this country was the very understandable anti-British reaction that followed. The formerly brisk trade in English racehorses all but stopped for a few years, so the horses that were lost through death and confiscation were not immediately replaced. There was also an anti-Church of England backlash. As we said, the Church of England did not disapprove of racing; in fact, the English clergy often owned racehorses. But as the Americans turned away in anger from the Church of England after the bitter fight, they embraced the more rigid, more puritan religions, and racing lost favor.

None of this lasted indefinitely, however, and after the brief cutoff, the Americans began trading with England again. Their crops, like tobacco, brought high prices, and soon the Southerners especially were ordering their agents in England to pick out good racehorses for them. Eventually, the traffic of racehorses from England to America reached a higher point than ever.

Toward the end of the 1700s many of the best imports were descendants of the Darley, the Byerly, and the Godolphin. Many, in fact, were sons or daughters of Herod, Matchem, and Eclipse, and *their* descendants would one day be registered Thoroughbreds. Again, many imposters were included in this near tidal wave of importations. This doesn't necessarily mean that they were not good horses. It is quite possible that some of those with the phoniest pedigrees did more for American horse stock in general than some of the genuine breds, many of which were duds when it came to breeding true. It is certain that the native horse stock of America gradually improved in size and quality as the English imports began to influence it more and more.

The records of most of these imports no longer exist—if they ever did. But of those that are known, two English stallions were imported about this time that were so outstanding that all the others seem insignificant beside them. They were *Diomed and *Messenger, two stallions who would so strongly stamp their marks on the American racehorse that those marks would never fade away.

7

*Messenger

*MESSENGER was foaled in 1780, the same year that our other wonder horse, *Diomed, won the first English Derby, so he was three years younger than *Diomed. To find our place in time even better, that same year Eclipse was sixteen years old, Herod twenty-two, and Matchem, at thirty-two, was living out his last days on earth. English racing had changed from mostly four-mile heat races for horses five years old and up to include shorter distances for younger horses. Across the Atlantic, the former colonists had forgiven the British and were once again buying English racehorses as fast as they could pay for them, especially in the Southern states. Up North, horse racing had not yet fully recovered its former popularity, though—a situation that *Messenger and his get were to change drastically. There were only twenty years left in the century, and much was to happen to the bred horse before it ended.

One of the best things that happened was *Messenger, whose unique and vital role in the development of the American racehorse began long before he was foaled, in his pedigree. His sire line consists of one great horse after another.

*Messenger, a gray colt, was sired by Mambrino, he by Engineer, he by Sampson, he by Blaze, he by Flying ("Mile-a-Minute") Childers, and he by the Darley. The Darley, of course, never raced. Flying Childers we remember, too—the fastest horse of his time. Blaze, the son of Childers, while his sire line was irreproachable, had a murky female line, with several unknowns close up. We do know that many of Blaze's descendants became Hackneys—fine harness horses that trotted and paced—and this would indicate that many of his ancestors also trotted and paced.

Blaze's son, Sampson, was not a true bred, therefore. Moreover, Sampson sired Shales, a great progenitor of the future trotting-pacing breed, the Standardbred. Sampson himself was a running horse and a great one, winning many a four-mile heat under tremendous weights. But he didn't look like a racehorse. At 15.2, he was large for his day and extremely heavy boned. When he appeared at the racecourses, the stable men joked about the "coach horse" come to race, so coarse was he. Sampson soon put a stop to the insults in the best possible way, by winning; but even so, he never became a popular racehorse sire because of the well-known fact that his dam's line lacked running blood and because his get inherited his coarseness and "lack of the true running type."

One of his sons, named Engineer, foaled in 1755, was a better-than-most racehorse, but his real claim to fame came from his best son, Mambrino, foaled in 1768.

Mambrino was a "great, strong-boned gray horse." His dam was a daughter of Cade and therefore a granddaughter of the fabled Godolphin, so he had no reason to be ashamed of his pedigree. Mambrino had two pacing crosses in this pedigree, though. His great-granddam, the beautiful Roxanna, was sired by Bald Galloway, one of the famous "pacing Galloways." The other cross, of course, was in his sire line, from Blaze on down.

Mambrino, °Messenger's sire, began racing when he was five years old, at long distances, under heavy weights, and often. He raced courageously and well. It is said that "he was on the track most of the time for five or six years" before he finally broke down under the great strain.

While Mambrino went on to sire a few good running horses, he never sired anything so good as himself. He was a successful sire of hunters and road horses, though, and an authority writing in 1805 went so far as to claim of Mambrino that "from his blood the breed of horses for the coach was brought nearly to perfection." This would mean good strong stylish horses with a "big trot." The same can be said of Mambrino's son °Messenger and his relationship to the Standardbred and to the coach horses of America. It might be mentioned here that Mambrino was highly exceptional for a bred in that while he could and did win many running races, his owner is reported to have offered to race him at a trot as well. A horse with great speed at both gaits is extremely unusual.

°Messenger, his greatest son, was also a strong, heavy-boned gray horse. Since artists tend to depict great horses as being beautiful, true or not, we really can't be sure exactly what he looked like. Some eyewitnesses say he was beautiful, while others admit to a certain coarseness, particularly about the head. All agree, however, that he was a tremendously strong horse with a remarkably large windpipe and "hips and quarters incomparably superior to all others."

°Messenger went to the races in England as a three-year-old in 1783 and raced for two years, winning some and losing some. He seems to have been more successful at shorter distances, up to two miles, and to have been beaten at the longer ones. His owner had a large stable, at any rate, and didn't enter *Messenger in any of the important races.

Then, after racing for only two years, *Messenger "disappeared"—as far as any records are concerned. The next we hear of him is in a stud advertisement in the May 27, 1788, *Pennsylvania Packet*, which began: "JUST IMPORTED—The capital, strong, full-blooded, English stallion, MESSENGER." It went on to say that this newly imported stallion would be standing to mares at "the sign of the Black Horse, in Market Street, Philadelphia, at the very low price of three guineas each mare, and one dollar to the groom." Then it mentions *Messenger's "so very great" racing record but does not say who imported the horse, or who his owner was then.

*Messenger's story continues to be uncertain and ill recorded. If he really was "JUST IMPORTED" in 1788, he was eight years old. And since the Englishman's favorite method of getting rid of an unwanted horse was to palm it off on an American, doubtless *Messenger's English stud career had been no more brilliant than his racing career, regardless of the advertisement's claims. Again we turn to Mr. Wallace, who for many years made an intensive search for the truth about *Messenger.

About no horse has so much been written and so little really known. . . . As a specimen of the admiration he excited, it has been told a hundred times that when the horse came cavorting down the gangplank from the ship, with a groom hanging onto each side of his head, literally carrying them some distance before he could be checked, an enthusiastic horseman shouted out, "There, in that horse a million dollars strikes the American soil."

This story has been told so often, even in England, that no doubt many people believe the startling prophecy was actually uttered. . . . Some said he was imported in 1785, while others dribbled along through the intermediate years till 1800 was fixed upon with great positiveness as the precise year.

There was even speculation years later as to whether *Messenger was imported into Philadelphia or New York. About that Mr. Wallace said:

I became satisfied, years before, that *Messenger made his first appearance in this country at Philadelphia, and that he was imported into that city instead of New York. In that view all the writers of the whole country were opposed to me . . .

Whereupon Mr. Wallace went to Philadelphia, started his search through the records, and found the advertisement of 1788 that verified his opinion.

*Messenger's life in America, as we said, however, was not recorded very well. It seems probable that he was taken from Philadelphia during the yellow-fever epidemic there a few years after his importation. And there seems to be evidence that he was sold to Henry Astor of New York in 1791. Thereafter, he was bought by the well-known race-horse owner, Cornelius Van Ranst, and stood at stud in and around New York City and Long Island the rest of his life.

Most of the mares brought to *Messenger's court were of the "native stock" variety, that is, loaded with pacing and trotting blood, and since *Messenger also carried plenty of the same, it is not surprising that his progeny became highly prized as road horses. Since these horses also proved to possess speed, it's not surprising either that eventually they would be raced. The ultimate outcome, the Standardbred, is the fastest trotting and pacing horse in the world.

Because *Messenger is best known as a founder of the Standardbred, his importance to the American Thoroughbred is sometimes overlooked. Because of his location in road-horse country, he had little opportunity to prove himself as a sire of running horses, too, but he managed to do just that. It would be his running sons and daughters, in fact, like Mambrino II and Miller's Damsel, that would revive the interest in racing in New York and bring it once again to a fever pitch.

Miller's Damsel, in particular, would win glory in two ways—first as the undisputed champion of the New York turf scene, and, even more important, as the dam of the literally unbeatable four-miler, American Eclipse.

Thus *Messenger, an English castoff, holds the remarkable honor of being a vital force in the development of two different breeds of horses. By the time he died on Long Island, twenty-eight years old, in 1808, he had almost all by himself rebuilt racing in the North, and founded a new breed as well.

Meanwhile, in 1798, another English castoff, *Diomed, had followed *Messenger across the ocean, coming ashore in Virginia. There this winner of the first English Derby would proceed to found a fantastic dynasty of Thoroughbreds that would rule the South for many generations to come.

8

*Diomed

*DIOMED'S STORY begins believably enough with his three-year-old win in the first Derby of 1780, but from there it takes on a melodramatic Cinderella-like quality that borders on fantasy. After his initial win, *Diomed raced brilliantly for a while and was compared favorably with Eclipse. But he seems to have broken down at an early point in his racing career; when brought back after a lay-up, he could no longer win consistently. His owner, Mr. Bunbury, put him to stud.

He became known among English horsemen as a bad sire, and his stud fee, never high, kept dropping until, when he was twenty-one years old, it had gone down to a shameful two guineas, with no customers even at that. At this point Mr. Bunbury probably decided he could better use the stall space, and he told his agent to see if he could sell the worthless old horse.

In Virginia at that time was a Colonel Hoomes who had been importing English racehorses and whose English agent was always on the lookout for a good buy for him. Hearing that the old *Diomed was up for sale, Hoomes inquired about him. His agent replied, warning him that *Diomed was a "tried and proved bad foal getter," and historians seem undecided now as to exactly what he meant by that, some claiming that *Diomed "got bad foals," others interpreting it as meaning that at his advanced age he was nearly or completely impotent. In any case, the agent also advised the Virginian and his partner, John Tayloe, not to "put any mares to him."

Why, after such a bad reference, Colonel Hoomes went ahead and bought the stallion anyway can only be guessed at. Perhaps he couldn't resist a bargain: a Derby winner for $250. It is also said that Hoomes and Tayloe had just lost one of their breeding stallions and needed another to meet their obligations to mare owners. And, even at his age, *Diomed was still an impressive-looking horse, about sixteen hands high and well built.

Whatever, he was purchased, and over to Virginia he came, gray hairs and all. The New World agreed with him. He immediately disproved any impotency ideas and started turning out one fine high-class foal after another. In a very short time he had made a name for himself, and Colonel Hoomes soon sold him for a reported $1,500—a good-sized fortune in those days and not a bad profit at any time.

But the new owner got a bargain, too, because for ten more years, a whole decade, the "used up, worthless old horse" kept on producing great racehorses, including, when he was thirty and only one year from his death, the fabulous mare Haynie's Maria, who drove Andrew Jackson wild with envy.

Andrew Jackson was a tyrant who was accustomed to

having his own way. He was also a great racing enthusiast. So when Haynie's Maria, then a three-year-old in 1811, distanced one of Jackson's horses, he was determined to buy her or beat her. Since Maria's trainer had a grudge against Jackson and would not sell her, "Old Hickory" began his long campaign to find a horse that was faster. The War of 1812 was a nuisance, interfering as it did with his racing, but from the battlefield Jackson told Colonel Johnson, "the Napoleon of the Turf," to find him "the best four-mile horse in Virginia, without regard to price."

Johnson did, in a horse called Pacolet, but Pacolet hurt his fetlock before he could challenge Maria. Jackson seethed at this setback and bought three more horses, all with the best reputations. One of these also got hurt, and Maria merrily romped away from the other two. Jackson raged when the bad news reached him on the battlefield. Then he had an idea. Maria obviously couldn't be beaten at four miles. But Jackson owned a mare noted for her sprinting abilities, so he challenged Maria to a half-mile dash. He couldn't lose! Or could he? Maria was never even headed, won by a good ten lengths, and Jackson lost $1,500—and his temper.

Really obsessed now, a week later Jackson borrowed a horse. Maria beat it in a canter. The next attempt was at two miles, with Maria giving Jackson's horse a 120-yard start. Maria fooled around, following for about a mile, then felt one touch of the spur, turned on, and won by 180 yards!

Jackson finally had to give up, but he never forgave or forgot. Much later, after a tremendously successful and eventful life, he was asked if he had ever met with a failure. He replied pensively, "Nothing that I can remember, except Haynie's Maria—I could not beat her."

Of *Diomed's hundreds of sons and daughters, the greatest of them all was Sir Archy, sometimes honored by the title "the Godolphin of America." Sir Archy's influence on the American Thoroughbred was second only to that of one other stallion: his own sire, *Diomed. When the old patriarch died in 1808 (the same year that *Messenger died), he left behind him in Sir Archy a sire of such enormous prepotence and popularity that it would one day be said that the racehorses of this country were "all of one blood": *Diomed's, through Sir Archy.

Sir Archy was foaled in 1805 in Cumberland County, Virginia. His dam was *Castianira, an imported blind mare. As was true of so many of our greatest horses, the colt did not attract any special attention at first. He was sired by the already famous *Diomed, yes, but so were countless other very fine horses. He was sold by his breeder as a two-year-old to Ralph Wormeley IV, who gave him the name Sir Archy. But by the time Sir Archy was old enough to race, Mr. Wormeley had lost interest in racing and tried to sell the young stallion. There were no buyers, strangely enough, even though he was "a fraction over 16 hands high, vigorous, clean-limbed and swift, of ideal proportions." Maybe it was just a bad year to sell horses. Anyway, Mr. Wormeley still owned Sir Archy (if reluctantly) when the three-year-old colt's first race came up.

Sir Archy should not have run in that race at all; he was still weakened from a recent bout with distemper. But his owner ran him rather than pay the forfeit for scratching him. Not surprisingly, the recuperating colt was distanced. A short time later he tried again but did little better, being beaten by True Blue, a horse owned by William Ransom Johnson.

Johnson was the most famous turf figure of his time. He was a renowned horseman and a state legislator while still a very young man, and he first proved his really superior knowledge of racehorses in 1807 to 1808 when his horses ran 63 races and *won* 61 of them, an incredible record. As shrewd as they came, he was nonetheless so completely respected that, as "the Napoleon of the Turf," his word and his advice became virtually law all over the South. And so honest was he that rival owners often turned their horses over to him to be trained and managed from his Virginia estate, perfectly sure that their horses would receive the same care and attention as Johnson's own. He was a sportsman in the best and truest sense of that word.

It was this man whose horse beat Sir Archy in his second race at the Washington track and this man who immediately after the race bought Sir Archy for $1,500, right then and there.

Then one of those curious things that happen in horse trading took place. Colonel Johnson raced the four-year-old Sir Archy the next year, and, healthy now and under the best trainer in the country, he did very well. Whereupon Colonel Johnson sold him for $5,000 to General William R. Davie. This may well have been the only mistake Johnson ever made, but it was a big one.

However, so greatly esteemed was Colonel Johnson's opinion that when he announced that Sir Archy was the best horse he'd ever seen, everyone took him at his word and declined to race a horse against him. Therefore, what may have been the fastest racehorse yet in America was retired to stud after only two years of racing for want of competitors.

It was just as well, for Sir Archy's greatness, like *Diomed's, would be as a sire. His blood was so intensely inbred for many years (like *Diomed, he was constantly bred and rebred to his own daughters and granddaughters) that what had been said about the racehorses of America being of one blood became even truer. During the first half of the 1800s the Southern racehorse especially became almost entirely Sir Archy stock, for the intense inbreeding went on for generations. The importing of English race-horses had stopped again with the War of 1812 and did not resume until about 1830, so there was no fresh blood coming in for a while. Ordinarily, this much inbreeding would produce weaknesses eventually, but so powerful was the blood of *Diomed and Sir Archy that it overcame any weaknesses, and the Sir Archy horses merely got better and better. These horses were so fast that by the time Sir Archy died in 1833 some of the big races from Washington on up northward would be closed to "Virginia, Maryland, and North Carolina horses" (almost all Sir Archy horses) because they were considered unbeatable.

Two of Sir Archy's very best sons were Timoleon, who would later sire the famous Boston, from whom sprang the incomparable Lexington; and Duroc, the sire of American Eclipse.

And, with American Eclipse, Colonel William Ransom Johnson, and Sir Archy's get, the characters were all present, and the stage was set for the most fantastic horse race in American history.

9

The Great North-South Race of 1823

Until this time, although New York had its new Union Course on Long Island, and racing up North had gradually regained respectability and popularity, the South had been the undisputed "cradle" of the American Thoroughbred, chiefly because of *Diomed and Sir Archy. The South was definitely the king of the American turf.

Then one horse changed all that. His name was American Eclipse, and like his English name bearer, he was undefeated. His owner, Mr. Van Ranst, gives us the best description of the horse.

He is a chestnut horse, with a star and the near hind foot white; 15 hands 3 inches high; possessing a large share of bone and muscle, and excelling all the racers of the day in the three great essentials of speed—courage, stoutness or lastingness, and ability to carry weight. He was foaled on the 25th of May, 1814, at

Dosoris, Long Island, on the farm of the late General Nathaniel Coles . . . at five months old, while a suckling, he gave his owner such a sample of stride, strength, and speed, that he was at that time named American Eclipse. He was sired by Duroc; his dam Miller's Damsel by *Messenger.

American Eclipse, carrying the best of both Northern and Southern bloodlines, certainly lived up to his early promise. His racing career consisted of one easy victory after another at the four-mile distance. It was his fifth race, however, that got the South's back up. On November 20, 1822, American Eclipse (a Northern horse) met Sir Charles, one of Sir Archy's fastest sons, on the Washington track and in a single four-mile heat actually had the gall to beat the Southern horse "with great ease."

As one authority, Charles E. Trevathan, said:

This defeat of Sir Charles . . . was the immediate incident which brought forth the challenge to Eclipse, and which resulted in the first national affair which the American turf had known. An offer was made at the Jockey Club dinner after the defeat of Sir Charles—the North vs. the South.

At this suggestion of the Southerners, a Northerner went them one better. He was John C. Stevens, a prominent New York horseman, and he counterchallenged the South—"the Napoleon of the Turf," etc.—to bring any Southern horse they chose to the Union Course the following spring, and American Eclipse would beat it, four-mile heats, $20,000 a side. Furthermore, the Southerners would not even have to choose which horse to run until the last minute, at the post.

What he was saying—and what the Southerners could not believe they were hearing—was an "Eclipse against the world" challenge.

Such arrogance from up North was, of course, not to be

borne. The challenge was immediately and confidently accepted, and "Napoleon" Johnson and the other Southern horsemen spent the winter choosing and collecting and conditioning the best the South could offer, which was very good, indeed. In May 1823, they started North with five formidable racehorses, four sired by Sir Archy and one his grandson.

Bad luck beset the Southerners immediately. Their first choice, a horse named John Richards, went lame in a trial race, shortly followed by another named Washington. When the troop arrived at the Union Course a few days before the big race, they had three horses left. Then came more bad luck. Colonel Johnson was such a notable and popular figure that New Yorkers outdid themselves to entertain him, and on the very eve of the race "Napoleon" himself was undone by all the wining and dining. The big day found him flat on his back in bed with a severe case of "colic," and the Southern contingent was without its leader and manager. The importance of this may be realized when it is recalled that a race of three four-mile heats required management. How the race was ridden—when to hold back, when to let out, and so forth, shouted from trackside—was the most vital aspect of it. And it was this crucial advice the Southerners lost when "Napoleon" succumbed to too many lobsters.

Then they lost one more horse to lameness, and when the time came, they had a choice between the remaining two: Betsey Richards and Sir Henry, both sired by Sir Archy. No one, not even the Southerners, knew until post time which horse they would run.

Meanwhile, during the preceding winter, the entire country had gone mad over this race.

From the very beginning of the colonies, with the North and the South settled by two such different types of people (the puritans and the cavaliers), there had been a certain amount of uneasiness between the two regions. The South resented and suspected the "money-grubbing, sharp-dealing Yankee." The Yankee, for his part, resented the Southern colonel's easier life and especially its basis, the slavery of human beings.

These simmering rivalries and suspicions often, in the early 1800s, reached their most violent peaks in the frequent "discussions" of the relative merits of Southern and Northern racehorses, discussions sometimes settled by pistols.

Thus it was inevitable that as the North began to lose its puritan inhibitions about racing and produced more and better racehorses, the rivalry increased proportionately.

This competition, followed by the North's unbearably arrogant challenge, was what set off the fireworks. The wild, widespread wagering on the coming North-South race reached staggering proportions over the winter, expressing not only loyalty to a horse but much more, loyalty to "our side." Banks in both sections became extremely jittery as many of them were actually cleaned out of cash when, to bet on the race, depositors withdrew all they had and then borrowed more if they could. When people ran out of cash and credit, they put up their livestock, their clothes, their slaves, even their plantations. One typical Southerner bet his whole tobacco crop for the next five years on whatever horse Colonel Johnson decided to run. He didn't even know what horse he was betting on.

By the day of the race the bettors, the banks, and the investment firms all awaited the results anxiously. It was all too clear by then that after the race either the North or the South would be facing a huge financial crisis. But both sides, even the South in spite of bad luck, were sure they would win.

Nobody was so sure, however, that he didn't want to know the results as soon as possible. The Union Course out on Long Island was several miles from New York City, and although the road to the track was packed solidly with travelers all that day, there wasn't room for everyone. Those waiting back in the city were to receive word by a system of signals. After each four-mile heat, a flag would be run up, and then horsemen would relay the news back to the city. A white flag would mean that American Eclipse had won the heat, a black flag would indicate a victory for the Southern horse.

Estimates of the attendance at the track that day run as high as 60,000. The crowd was immense. Among the excited mob were the Vice-President of the United States (sent by the President, who felt it improper to attend himself); Andrew Jackson, who in six years would be President; almost every other important man in the country; in fact, adjourned for the great occasion, the entire Congress of the United States was there.

The fervid betting continued right up till post time, when the South brought Sir Henry to the post. This son of Sir Archy looked a great deal like his opponent Eclipse—a chestnut with a star and a white foot, somewhat smaller. Sir Henry was only four years old and therefore was required to carry only 108 pounds, while the nine-year-old Eclipse carried 126. Sir Henry was ridden by Walden, Eclipse by Crafts.

The first four-mile heat was wildly exciting, run at a killing pace the entire distance, with Walden keeping Sir Henry under a hard pull most of the way and American Eclipse being cruelly whipped and spurred by Crafts. A contemporary writer, an eyewitness to the event, wrote an account of it later for the *Turf Register*, signing himself only, "An Old Turfman." He said, concerning the end of this first heat:

When they passed me about the commencement of the stretch, seventy to eighty rods from home, the space between them was about sixteen feet, or a full length and a half in the clear. [Sir Henry leading.] Here the rider of Henry turned his head round, and took a view for an instant of his adversary; Walden used neither whip nor spur; but maintained a hard and steady pull, under which his horse appeared accustomed to run. Crafts continued to make free use of the whip; his right hand in so doing was necessarily disengaged from the bridle, his arm often raised high in the air, his body thrown abroad, and his seat loose and unsteady; not having strength to hold and gather his horse with one hand and at the same time keep his proper position; in order to acquire a greater purchase, he had thrown his body quite back to the cantle of the saddle, stuck his feet forward by way of bracing himself with the aid of the stirrups, and in this style he was belaboring his horse, going into the last quarter . . . From this place to the winning post, Eclipse gained by a few feet, Henry coming in ahead about a length in the clear. The shortest time of this heat, as returned by the judges on the stand, was 7 minutes, 37½ seconds.

I pushed immediately up to the winning post, in order to view the situation of the respective horses, after this very trying and severe heat; for it was in fact running the whole four miles. Sir Henry was less distressed than I had expected to find him; Eclipse also bore it well, but of the two he appeared the most jaded; the injudicious manner in which he had been ridden had certainly annoyed and unnecessarily irritated him; . . . Crafts, in using his whip wildly, had struck him too far back, and had cut him not only upon his sheath, but had made a deep incision upon his testicles . . . The blood flowed profusely from both of these foul cuts . . . The incapacity of Crafts to manage Eclipse—who required much urging, and at the same time to be pulled hard—was apparent to all.

This first heat raises a question: Why would such an obviously inept and cruel rider be chosen to ride in such an important race? The answer is just as obvious: Eclipse was not meant to win the first heat. And when the odds on Sir Henry immediately went up to three-to-one, the Yankees' purpose was achieved.

The black flag was run up, and the poised riders relayed the bad news back to the city; the stock market collapsed.

After a half-hour rest, the second heat started—with a new rider for Eclipse, Mr. Purdy. It seems to us today that Purdy was hardly less brutal than Crafts had been, being almost as free with the whip and spur, but those were brutal times, and at least Purdy knew how to ride Eclipse, having ridden him often before.

The second heat was as nip and tuck as the first one. Both horses had recovered well, were still full of run, and kept the pace a blistering one. Sir Henry again led until they got into the last mile when, again going to our eyewitness:

Purdy seized, with a quickness and dexterity peculiar to himself, the favorable moment . . . made a dash at him accordingly, and passed him on the left! . . . Just as they had finished the bend and entered upon the straight run . . . Eclipse for the first time was fairly and clearly ahead. He now with the help of the persuaders, which were freely bestowed, kept up his run, and continued gradually, though slowly, to gain during the remaining three-quarters of a mile, and came in about two lengths ahead. As they passed up the stretch . . . the shouting, clapping of hands, waving of handkerchiefs, long and loud applause sent forth by the Eclipse party exceeded all description; it seemed to roll along the track as the horses advanced, resembling the loud and reiterated shout of contending armies . . .

As well it might. These two great, game horses had just completed eight miles, running nearly full out the whole time, and had completed the second heat in a remarkable 7 minutes, 49 seconds!

This time the white flag went up, but so close was the contest that the betting on both sides never wavered. The Southern contingent decided to change riders on Sir Henry for this third, decisive heat and put up Arthur Taylor, "a trainer of great experience, and long a rider equaled by few and surpassed by none." The Southerners' strategy changed, too. It soon became apparent that Taylor's orders were to hang back this time, to let Eclipse lead and set the pace, saving Henry for the finish.

But Purdy, on Eclipse, was also an experienced rider. When he saw Taylor's intention, such faith did he have in Eclipse's stamina that he pushed Eclipse hard right from the start to make Sir Henry, "if determined to trail, employ all his strength and speed without keeping anything in reserve for the run in." To continue our witness's description:

Sir Henry continued to trail, apparently under a pull, never attempting to come up, until they had both fairly entered the straight run towards the extermination of the last mile, and had advanced within about sixty rods from home. Here Sir Henry being about five yards behind, made a dash, and ran up to Eclipse, so far as to cover his quarters or haunch with his head, and for a moment had the appearance of going ahead; he made a severe struggle for about two hundred yards, when he again fell in the rear, and gave up the contest.

The white flag ran up; the stock market jumped up. Several Southerners, having lost everything they had, killed themselves right on the spot, and the "Great North-South Race of 1823" was over. Sir Henry had gallantly met the North's challenge, but from now on the South could no longer claim complete superiority in breeding Thoroughbreds.

Sir Henry and American Eclipse had run twelve miles that day, none of it "loafing," in 23 minutes, an average time of 1 minute, 59 seconds each mile. A good modern Thoroughbred can do a mile in about 1:37, but that is just one mile, not one out of twelve. Those four-milers were real racehorses.

"The Napoleon of the Turf," Colonel Johnson, immediately challenged the North to a rematch "for any sum from twenty to fifty thousand dollars," any horse they cared to run. The North, represented by John C. Stevens, wisely turned down the offer. The country's economy could scarcely stand another such race so soon. It would be, in fact, nearly twenty years before the next North-South race, when Boston would meet Fashion in 1842.

But only three years later, the blood of American Eclipse (*Messenger) and Sir Henry (Sir Archy) would meld in producing the most famous mare of the American turf. Her name was Black Maria.

10

Black Maria

On June 15, 1826, Black Maria was foaled in New York. Her sire was American Eclipse, and her dam was Lady Lightfoot, a famous racing daughter of Sir Archy. In spite of this splendid pedigree, at first it seemed that the little black filly was doomed, for when she was only two days old, Lady Lightfoot died "from the effects of a violent cold." Somehow the tiny foal survived, and went on to do considerably more than merely survive. A description in the *Turf Register* of 1832 reads: "Her color is indicated by her name, and her great size, strength and stride show her a worthy daughter of a noble sire." A far cry from the puny little orphan of five years before!

This big black mare, though rich in Sir Archy blood, was definitely a Northern horse. Foaled in Harlem, her entire racing career took place in and around New York City. And it was a career of great hardship and endurance.

Her owner, the same John Stevens who was American Eclipse's "principal" in the North-South Race, scarcely ever let her rest. She was a great favorite, attracting huge crowds whenever she ran, and rather than disappoint her fans, Stevens always ran her whether she was fit or not. In those days, when a race was set up, a prize or purse was established, and another sum, usually about half that of the purse, was set as the forfeit in the event of a horse being entered and then withdrawn. And Stevens boasted that he had never paid a forfeit and never would as long as his horse could walk. (This was considered "sporting," not cruel.) Therefore, while Black Maria lost twelve of her twenty-five starts, it was only because she was often run when her trainer, had Stevens bothered to consult him, would not have allowed it. Black Maria was literally raced to death.

Her potential was instantly recognized in her very first race as a three-year-old. It was a "produce match" (what is now called a futurity), a race set up before either entry was foaled, actually a race between American Eclipse's daughter and Sir Archy's son, a brown colt named Brilliant, owned by Colonel Johnson.

Although Black Maria had never before been on the track, Colonel Johnson's hawk eye immediately realized that the black filly was special. The race had been set up for $5,000 a side and $2,500 forfeit, and as soon as Colonel Johnson saw the filly, he offered to pay $1,750 to take his colt back home. The offer was not accepted, though, and rather than pay the full forfeit, Colonel Johnson stayed and watched Black Maria beat Brilliant in two heats.

Three long, hard years later, the much-raced, mismanaged, but extremely popular mare would run her greatest race, a race that would give her name immortality. This was the Jockey Club Purse of 1832, on the Union Course, four-mile heats.

First a little more about these "four-milers." We have seen why generalship—the management of the race—was so important at those great distances. We watch a race now that is finished in less than two minutes. One heat in those old races lasted for seven to eight minutes, with more heats to follow. And seven or eight minutes is a long time to race. During that time, in a field of half a dozen other horses, the leader might be challenged several times. These challenges were called "making a dash at the leader," or "brushes," and during them the leader was forced to run flat out. That, combined with racing at a good clip the entire distance, could easily wear a horse down to the point where another horse, which had more or less taken it easy for three or three and a half miles, could suddenly turn on and win over the exhausted leader. Tremendous stamina was required of all the horses, and especially one that did much "leading the field."

By 1832, Black Maria had raced for four years and was acknowledged to be a great endurance mare, but was not thought to have great speed. In this, her finest race, however, she proved that she had phenomenal quantities of both.

It had been raining, and the track was wet and heavy, making stamina even more important than usual. Four horses started: Black Maria, Lady Relief, Slim, and the famous mare Trifle.

According to the *Turf Register*, the first heat went as follows:

At the tap of the drum, the four went off well together, Relief taking the lead within the first quarter, followed closely by Slim, then by Trifle, and last but not least by Black Maria. The first mile indicated a waiting race, as all the riders had their horses under the hardest pull, each seeming desirous that his antagonists should take the lead. Trifle, impatient with such trifling, began to make play, and this aroused Black Maria, who was trailing along quietly behind the whole. With a few huge strides she brought herself to the front, passed the whole before she came to the judges' stand, followed closely by the gallant little Trifle, who "stuck to her" like an accompanying phantom. At the beginning of the third mile the leading nags made play, and during the whole of it Maria held the lead, followed closely by Trifle, while Relief and Slim were (as we believe, not willingly) at a most respectable distance in the rear.

After passing the judges' stand and entering upon the fourth mile . . . Trifle "made a dash" at Maria and ran her so hard down the descending ground upon the straight side that [Black Maria] gave up the track, which was taken up by the Southern lady [Trifle] and kept with apparent ease round the turn. . . . Here, at a moment when all opinions had given Trifle the heat as a safe thing . . . Maria went at her, and before you could count one she shot by Trifle and won the heat with ease, there being a considerable gap between herself and Trifle, and a much greater one between the latter and the hindmost horses.

In the very first heat, on this slow, heavy track, Maria already showed not only that she was game but that she had speed to match the best of them. This she continued to prove all that long afternoon, as one heat followed another. In the second one, because of a mistake made by her rider, she failed to win, but "dead heated" (tied) with Trifle. In the third heat—the ninth, tenth, eleventh, and twelfth miles of this cruelly hard race—she was challenged by the relatively fresh Lady Relief, and then her rider lost his head again and let Trifle beat her in a last-second dash under the wire.

The race, then, with Black Maria winning the first heat, a dead heat for the second, and Trifle winning the third, still had no victor. A fourth heat was asked of these tired, gallant horses.

Again Lady Relief, who for the most part of the previous twelve miles had pretty much taken it easy, came to life in the last mile of the fourth heat and in a desperate challenge beat Black Maria, both mares hard under the whip.

It doesn't seem possible to us today that any of these mares, after sixteen miles of racing on a heavy track, could even walk—especially Black Maria, who had been pushed by first one challenger and then another the entire distance, with no chance to loaf along anywhere in the race. Having run the hardest of them all, in fact, Black Maria would seem to have been the least likely one to have enough strength left to win the fifth heat now necessary.

But Black Maria did come back, and she earned once and for all her place in horse history. Not only did she have the strength and the courage to run these last four miles of a twenty-mile race, she "took hold of them in the twentieth mile of the race and . . . carried them so fast that she stopped them dead and came along home . . . winning without the touch of a whip or spur!"

Black Maria is what horsemen mean when they say a Thoroughbred has heart. From that moment on she was famous, both North and South, as "the Twenty-Mile Mare." She continued to race under the heavy hand of Mr. Stevens until she was nine years old and done in. Then her life began its happy ending when she retired to a much-deserved rest in Tennessee. There Black Maria produced many fine foals, making her mark in the Stud Book as well as on the turf.

11

The Gray Eagle-
Wagner Races

I T WAS about Black Maria's time that "the West"—Kentucky and Tennessee—came into its own. The famous strip of bluegrass that runs through those states and its settlers' devotion to racing made its supremacy of the American turf inevitable. Equally inevitable was the growing rivalry between Kentucky and the states to the south. This rivalry came to a head most memorably when Gray Eagle met Wagner.

Wagner, a son of Sir Charles, was the standard bearer for Tennessee and Louisiana. A blaze-faced chestnut, he was a five-year-old. Gray Eagle, "Kentucky's finest," was a gorgeous gray, sixteen hands high, sired by the good horse Woodpecker. Kentucky idolized him.

The autumn of 1839 saw these two giants meet for the first time at Louisville. All the previous year the race had been talked about constantly, and to say that feelings ran high is to put it mildly. The coming race had been nearly the only subject for discussion for months. An enormous, feverishly excited crowd gathered for the event, among them Henry Clay and other great men. Nobody who was anybody would have missed it for the world.

Once again we are fortunate in having an eyewitness account available, this one written by William T. Porter.

There were ten nominations to this stake, but only four came to the post . . . They were Wagner, Gray Eagle, Queen Mary, and Hawk-Eye.

Before the race, the horses were displayed to the fashionable assemblage with full pomp and ceremony.

All eyes were directed to a motley group approaching from Mr. Garrison's stable: "with stately step, and slow," Wagner, the proud champion of Louisiana, made his appearance. He was directly stripped, and a finer exhibition of the perfection to which the trainer's art can be carried we have rarely seen. His coat and eye were alike brilliant. Wagner is a light chestnut, with a roan stripe on the right side of his face, and white hind feet—about fifteen and a half hands high. His head is singularly small, clean and bony, set on a light but rather long neck; forehanded, he resembles the pictures of his sire, Sir Charles, and in his carriage is said to resemble him. His shoulder is immensely strong, running well back into a good middle piece, which is well ribbed home. One of the finest points about him is his great depth of chest; few horses can measure with him from the point of shoulder to the brisket . . . He has uncommonly strong and wide hips, a good loin, remarkably fine stifles and thighs, with as fine hocks and legs as ever stood under a horse. Wagner has been in training ever since his three-year-old form, and has traveled over three thousand miles, without three weeks' rest.

Since the site of the race was Louisville, Kentucky, Wagner's appearance was greeted politely but not hysterically. But when Gray Eagle appeared, the crowd welcomed its hero resoundingly.

As he came up in front of the stand, his lofty carriage and flashing eye elicited a burst of applause, which told better than words can express the intense and ardent aspirations felt in his success, by every son and daughter of Kentucky. Clinton, his trainer, immediately stripped off his sheet and hood, and a finer specimen of the high-mettled racer was never exhibited. He was in condition to run for a man's life—a magnificent gray, nearly sixteen hands high, with the step of a gazelle and the strength of a Bucephalus. Mr. Burbridge had told us that of one thing he was confident—his horse might want foot, but of his game he was certain.

Porter goes on to say that Gray Eagle had never yet lost a heat and to describe him as thoroughly as he described Wagner. Suffice it to say here that Gray Eagle was as well formed as Wagner, and even more beautiful.

Riding Wagner, the Southern entry, was "Cato," a well-known slave jockey, at nearly 110 pounds. Gray Eagle's jockey

lost the confidence of his owners just before the race, and at the eleventh hour they were obliged to hunt up another. Stephen Welch was selected, though obliged to carry 13 pounds deadweight in shot-pouches on his saddle! The friends of Gray Eagle, however, had entire confidence in his honesty; and it is clear that he did his best, though, weighing as he did but 82 pounds, he had neither the strength nor the stamina to hold and control a powerful, fiery horse like Gray Eagle.

The four horses were lined up and sent for the first heat.

Gray Eagle was the last off, while Wagner went away like a quarter-horse, with Queen Mary well up second; they were taken in hand at once. . . . With Gray Eagle still trailing . . . Wagner came first to the stand, and at the turn Cato having held up his whip as a signal to the . . . boys on Garrison's stable that "the old Sorrel Stud" was going just right, they gave him a slight cheer, at which Wagner broke loose, and made a spread eagle of the field in "no time." The other jockeys were not a little startled at this demonstration of Wagner's speed, and each called upon his nag, so that . . . the field closed. Stephen here let out Gray Eagle, and like twin bullets the gallant gray and Wagner came out of the melee . . . Stephen was told to "pull him steady," so that before Wagner reached the stand, Queen Mary had changed places with Gray Eagle, notwithstanding her saddle had slipped on her withers. Hawk-Eye was already in difficulty, and for him the pace was getting "no better very fast." Gray Eagle set to work in earnest on entering the back-stretch, first out-footing the Queen and then challenging Wagner. . . . At the half-mile post, Cato called upon Wagner, and, the critical moment having arrived, Stephen collared him with the gray, on the outside. For three hundred yards the pace was tremendous; Gray Eagle once got his head and neck in front, and a tremendous shout was sent up; but Wagner threw him off so far in going round the last turn that, halfway up the stretch, Mr. Burbridge ordered him to be pulled up, and Wagner won cleverly, Queen Mary dropping just within her distance [that is, just managing not to be distanced] . . . Hawk-Eye was nowhere. Time, 7:48.

The disappointment and mortification were so great that for the first twenty minutes after the heat Queen Mary was freely backed against Gray Eagle, while so far as Wagner was concerned, it was considered a "dead open and shut." Before the forty-five minutes had elapsed, however, a reaction took place in favor of Gray Eagle. *Not a Kentuckian on the ground laid out a dollar on Wagner!* From the first, the very few individuals who were disposed to back him on account of his blood, his form, his performances and his condition, had not staked a dollar; their judgment prompted them to back the Southern champion, but they *would not* bet against *Kentucky!*

Mr. Porter says all the horses cooled off well "but more especially Gray Eagle, who appeared not to mind the run a jot." Clinton, Gray Eagle's trainer, commented that they had "got a good scrape out of him," that he had sweated profusely, and this fact seemed to have helped Gray Eagle a good deal since Mr. Porter remarked that the horse seemed to move more freely after his heavy sweat.

The second heat was all Gray Eagle and Wagner, and a blistering one.

Stephen got Gray Eagle into straight work on the back side, he made play for the track, and after a terrific burst of speed for one hundred and fifty yards, he came in front; keeping up his stroke, he soon after made a gap of four lengths . . . Gray Eagle kept up his murderous rate throughout the entire second mile; Wagner lay up close, and there was no faltering, no flinching, no giving back, on the part of either. . . . Gray Eagle made the running to beyond the half-mile post on the third mile, and the pace seemed too good to last, but there were "links" yet to be "let out." From this time the two cracks made a match of it . . . Queen Mary was out of the race. Near the Oakland House Wagner set to work to do or die . . . "Rowel him up!" shouted his owner to Cato; while Garrison . . . was waving his hat to him to come on! The rally that ensued . . . was desperate, but Wagner could not gain an inch; as they swung round into the quarter stretch they were lapped . . . Both horses got a taste of steel and catgut . . . at the turn Stephen maneuvered so as to press Wagner on the outside, and soon after drew out clear in front; looking so much like a winner that the crowd . . . sent up a cheer that make the welkin ring for miles around. The group on Wagner's stable again bid him "go on!" but Cato, "calm as a summer's morning," was quietly biding his time. . . . Fully aware of the indomitable game of the nonpareil under him, he thought if he could bottle him up for a

Wagner, bred by Daniel Dugger of Virginia in 1834, and Leviathan, bred abroad in 1823. *Courtesy Kenneth M. Newman, The Old Print Shop, New York City.*

Lexington, granddad of Thoroughbreds.

Messenger, the great progenitor and founder of the American trotting horse.

"Eclipse," an oil painting by Francis Sartorius.

Horse racing in the 1700s.

Racehorses training in the 1700s.

Sir Barton, first Triple Crown Winner, 1919. *Wide World Photos.*

Gallant Fox, Triple Crown Winner, 1930. *Wide World Photos.*

few hundred yards there was still another run to be got out of him. He accordingly took a bracing pull on his horse, and though it was "go along" every inch, Wagner recovered his wind so as to come again at the head of the quarter-stretch. Stephen [the little 82-pounder] had become so exhausted as to be unable to give Gray Eagle the support he required; he rode wide, and was all abroad in his seat. From the Oakland House home it was a terrible race! By the most extraordinary exertions Wagner got up neck and neck with "the gallant gray" as they swung round the turn. . . . The feelings of the assembled thousands were wrought up to a pitch that was absolutely painful—silence the most profound reigned over that vast assembly, as these noble animals sped on as if life and death called forth their utmost energies. Both jockeys had their whip-hands at work, and at every stroke, each spur, with a desperate stab, was buried to the rowel head . . . Now Wagner, now Gray Eagle, had the advantage. It will be a dead heat! "See! Gray Eagle's got him!"—"No—Wagner's ahead!"—a moment ensues—the people shout—hearts throb—ladies faint—a thrill of emotion, and the race is over! Wagner wins by a neck, in 7:44, the best race ever run south of the Potomac; while Kentucky's gallant champion demonstrates his claim to that title by a performance which throws into the shade the most brilliant ever made in his native state.

The Kentuckians, of course, couldn't let it go at that. Gray Eagle had certainly been "gallant," but he had lost, and such a situation had to be rectified as soon as possible. They had seen how closely matched the two horses were, that Gray Eagle had lost as much to Cato's expert riding as to Wagner's speed. So when the Jockey Club purse came along five days later, with both horses entered, the crowd was bigger than before and just as hopeful. Cato again rode Wagner, and little Stephen Welch, when no one heavier could be found in time, again rode Gray Eagle.

The first heat of this second race was another heart-bursting, seesawing battle, this time with Gray Eagle being less than a length ahead at the finish. The time was 7:51, indicating that neither horse was running with all the stops out. The crowd naturally went wild with joy, having at last seen their champion show his heels to the Southern horse. Huge sums were wagered, with Gray Eagle now slightly favored.

The second heat was still another neck-and-neck struggle that kept the crowd on its feet with anxiety. Both horses showed again their unflinching courage, "always able to do a *little more.*" Again the battle seesawed, with one "desperate rush" following another. Toward the end of the fourth mile,

Both jockeys were nearly faint with their exertions, and Stephen, poor fellow, lost his presence of mind. Up to the distance stand it was impossible to say which was ahead; whips and spurs had been in constant requisition the entire mile, but at this moment Stephen gave up his pull, and unconsciously yawed his horse across the track, which broke him off his stride, while Cato, holding Wagner well together . . . , at length brought him through a gallant winner by a neck, having run the last mile in 1:48, and the heat in 7:43!

So each champion had won one heat, and the battle was not yet over. The horses and the jockeys having recovered, they came back to run the ninth-through-twelfth miles of the race—their second such race in one week. And tragedy struck.

At the word "Go!" they broke off with a racing stride, Wagner taking the lead by about two lengths; the pace was moderate, for Stephen on Gray Eagle was expressly charged to pull him steady and wait for orders. Wagner accordingly led with an easy stroke through the first mile, and being cheered as he passed the stand, he widened the gap soon after to four or five lengths. At the half-mile post Gray Eagle made play, and had nearly closed the gap . . . when he suddenly faltered as if shot, and after limping a step or two, abruptly stopped! "Gray Eagle has let down!" was the cry on all hands, and when the spectators became aware of the truth of the painful announcement, the tearful eyes . . . and the heartfelt sorrow . . . indicated the sincerity of the sympathy . . .

Soon after Gray Eagle was stopped, Cato pulled Wagner out of his stride, and galloped him slowly round. The intelligence of the High Mettled Racer was clearly indicated by Wagner's subsequent action; from the head of the stretch home he invariably went at a racing pace . . . frequently bursting off in spite of his rider. On the fourth mile . . . in spite of Cato's utmost exertions, he ran at the very top of his speed, as if plied with steel and whalebone the whole way! We never saw a more magnificent exhibition of unflinching game. Even the friends of Gray Eagle forgot their distress for a moment, in doing justice to the gallant and victorious champion of Louisiana.

The awesome duels between these two superb racehorses were indicative of two important points: that Kentucky, Tennessee, and Louisiana were fast gaining supremacy on the American turf; and that the rivalry between North and South was continuing without respite. In fact, it was growing more bitter every year. Many such North-South races were being hotly contested, and now we must do homage to the greatest of the South's contenders at that time, the stallion named Boston.

12

Boston

BOSTON SEEMS an odd name for the champion racehorse of the South until we discover how he got that name. There was a popular card game then called Boston, and the owner of the colt who named him had won him in such a game. The city of Boston had nothing to do with it.

In any event, the colt was foaled in Virginia in 1833. He was sired by Timoleon, one of Sir Archy's best sons, and therefore was yet another "great" in the line of old *Diomed. Sooner or later, of course, he fell into the company of "Napoleon" Johnson, who at first thought very little of the chestnut colt with the blaze face when he was being trained by John Belcher, one of Colonel Johnson's men.

He was a peculiar colt right from the first, but Belcher thought he "saw something in him." Johnson did not agree, and in all probability Boston would have wound up racing in the bush circuit farther south had not Belcher talked Johnson into watching a trial run one day.

Johnson had two good racers at the Petersburg track that morning, Argyle and Mary Blunt, and Belcher finally managed to get Johnson's reluctant permission to run the little no-account stud colt with them just to see what he would do. Things started out badly. Charles E. Trevathan says,

The two trial horses went away from Boston just as they pleased, and he seemed unable to keep within striking distance of them. Belcher was so disgusted that he gave Boston up, and turned away to escape the badinage of Colonel Johnson and the other trainer, Arthur Taylor. Argyle and Mary Blunt were running a fast trial head and head, and Boston was trailing far behind them when they turned into the head of the stretch at the end of the last mile. Then Boston did a most surprising thing; he suddenly put his head into the bridle and set himself to run. He showed such a marvelous burst of speed that he beat the pair of them through the stretch and finished first. Then Colonel Johnson said he would do.

That Boston "would do" was the understatement of the century. In nine years of racing Boston came to be considered "the best horse this side of the Atlantic." Because of his blaze face he was affectionately known as "Old White-Nose."

In 1837, Boston came under the direct management of Napoleon Johnson, and though for a while he was raced as second string to Johnson's other horses, he soon showed that he was not second-string material.

He remained a peculiar horse, that is, an individual with a mind of his own. Trevathan comments about one race, for instance: "Boston won the next two heats and the race, though he was so full of notions at the start of the third heat that he had to be whipped off from the post." What was he so "notional" about? The track was muddy, and he objected.

By 1839, Boston's reputation was such that "Boston was entered to start in a Jockey Club purse of $700 and Colonel Johnson was paid $500 not to start him, because his running would scare everything else out of the field and the race would be spoiled." The same thing happened a week later at another track. "Colonel Johnson received $500 of a thousand dollar purse to keep 'Old White-Nose' in the stable."

Every now and then the North would come up with a horse they thought might beat Boston, but every time he straightened them out very quickly. Outside of being paid off occasionally not to run, Boston's career remained a succession of victories and, when the other entries didn't dare show up, walkovers. Boston did lose once in a while, but only when he was raced while utterly out of condition.

In 1839, the year of the Wagner-Gray Eagle races "out West," Boston won every race he started in and "defeated every good horse racing north of the Potomac." If Colonel Johnson wanted revenge for his defeat by American Eclipse, Boston was certainly the horse to get it for him.

In 1840, there was almost no horse left considered to have a chance against him at the four-mile distance. Colonel Johnson took him down South. Trevathan wrote:

The various jockey clubs between Boston's home at Petersburg and the Union Course at Long Island were dismayed at the prospect of having their programmes ruined by the appearance of "Old White-Nose" and it was at their personal solicitation that Boston was withdrawn from all of these races and sent away to the South, that the sport of the North might not meet with such serious interference. The possibility was discussed of opening their races to the world, *"Bar Boston."*

How Napoleon must have enjoyed all this!

In the spring of 1841 Boston was retired. Like the English Eclipse, he had no worthy competition and so went to the stud at seven years old. He brought in $4,200 in stud fees that spring and summer, at $100 a mare. But neither Boston's owners nor his many fans really liked it. They missed seeing him run. So, unable to resist it, in the fall Colonel Johnson put the stallion back in training and started to work some of the fat off him. After reconditioning, he was given a trial run at Petersburg. A New Yorker, sent down to spy, reported to his friends that it was the fastest trial ever run in the fifty-year history of the Petersburg track. Obviously his summer vacation hadn't done Boston any harm.

Napoleon was gleeful—and superconfident. At once he challenged the world (meaning mostly, of course, the North). It was the wildest challenge yet: Boston at four-mile heats against *any two* horses for $45,000 a side; Boston to race both horses, first one, then the other in alternate heats. In other words, Napoleon was saying that Boston could outrun and outlast two horses, each only half as tired as he was. This offer is still the most wide open ever made.

And here we see once and for all what the American racing public thought of Boston. Here was a seven-year-old horse that had just been completely out of condition for a whole season. For $45,000 one would think that anyone with two decent racehorses would have accepted such a wild-eyed challenge. But such was Boston's reputation, such a giant of the turf was he, that no one did.

Napoleon eventually overplayed his hand, however, even with such a great horse. He started Boston racing again on September 30, 1841, and in the following 29 days subjected the newly reconditioned stallion to *five* four-mile heat races. Even a giant can falter if the burden is heavy enough.

Boston won the first four races, a remarkable feat. But the fifth was a disaster, still unexplained satisfactorily. Only a week before he had won "gallantly" and seemed in good shape in spite of his exhausting schedule. But when he met a horse named John Blount and a mare named Fashion on October 28, he could hardly gallop at all. His owners must have "known something" because for once they didn't bet a nickel on him. The public was aghast.

Nowadays we might at least suspect that he was doped, but more likely he was simply worn out and sulking. Colonel Johnson does not seem to have been the type to dope a horse even if he had had any reason to. At any rate, Boston ended his glorious 1841 racing season in ignominious defeat. But in his life, up to that date, he had won 35 of 38 races and nearly $50,000, which in 1841 was a tremendous sum.

Fashion, the mare, had beaten Boston unfairly. But when her owner accepted a challenge from Colonel Johnson to meet Boston again the following spring, she got her chance to try it again on fairer terms.

Fashion was the darling of the Northern tracks. Sired by *Trustee, an imported English horse, she was out of Bonnets o' Blue, a mare that had been a great favorite herself. Bonnets o' Blue had been sired by Sir Archy, out of Reality, and Reality, Colonel Johnson had once averred, was "the very best racehorse that I ever saw." So Fashion's credentials were in order, and she herself was a great racing mare.

Only four years old in 1842, she was a chestnut with a star, a ring of white around one hoof, and three "luck spots" on her right hip—dark spots such as those sported by many famous racehorses. About 15.2 hands, rich in color, her description compares most favorably with that of the ideal modern Thoroughbred: long-geared, rangy, high-withered, sleek, yet powerfully built where it counts. She was a fast, beautiful mare, and the public adored her.

She, too, had her peculiarities. Then, as now, most racehorses did best under a good steady pull, but Fashion, although a very spirited mare, raced fastest on a loose rein. Fortunately, she showed this odd trait early, and since the same boy, Joe Laird, always rode her, he had no problems with it. Mr. Trevathan says, in fact, that "in the supreme moments of contest when the vital question was to be asked; . . . it came known to the sportsmen of that day that when young Laird 'threw away his reins' Fashion might be expected to let out a most astounding burst of speed."

Since Fashion's trainer owned a public training stable in New Jersey with many other fine racers in it, she did not get all the chances to run she might have had in a private stable. Still, by 1842, only four years old, she had several good wins to her credit. After Boston sulked, or whatever he did, in that race we just described, she had gone on to "run the other horse, John Blount, to lameness."

Boston, then, would have his work cut out for him when he traveled north in the spring of 1842 to meet Fashion at the Union Course.

The mare came to the great race as fit as the proverbial fiddle. Boston's trainer, Arthur Taylor (who had ridden Sir Henry in the last "Great North-South Race") was muttering, however, that Boston could have stood more preparation for such a big race. Nonetheless, both parties were full of confidence as always, and the Great Race of 1842 was on, with Joe Laird up on Fashion and the famous jockey Gil Patrick riding Boston.

First heat: For three miles both horses ran well and fast. The enormous crowd (there had been violent riots when the railway system could not carry them all to the track) was so excited that it pushed onto the track itself, leaving only a narrow strip free for the horses to pass through. The screaming and cheering was deafening. At the start of the fourth mile Laird "shook the whip over her head," and Fashion, who had been following Boston slightly, put on an incredible flash of speed and passed the stallion. Amid the tremendous roar of the crowd Boston went to work, and on the backstretch he lapped her for a distance when Gil Patrick took him back and "bottled him up for a desperate brush up the hill."

But on the turn he cut so close to the fence that Boston struck his hip on a post, causing him to falter for an instant. Fashion was then ahead by three lengths, but around the turn Boston recovered his stride and closed up to within a few feet of the flying mare. At that point the crowd got entirely out of hand and nearly blocked the track.

Such was the racket made by "thousands of spectators, excited to the highest pitch," that both horses faltered at the noise and at the mob on the track in front of them. With only a quarter-mile left to go, both riders went to the whip freely. Emerging from the crowd, the two horses were very close, with Boston still a few feet behind. Then he nearly caught her, but someone in the crowd yelled to her rider, "Rouse up the mare! Boston's on you!" and Laird cut her with the whip. Responding valiantly, Fashion then "did her best," and in spite of Boston's mighty rush she crossed the finish line about a length to the good. The crowd, mostly New Yorkers, was hysterical. And the time of the four-mile heat was 7:32½, the fastest ever run in America by a good margin. Fashion, still only a filly, was certainly showing them what the weaker sex could do.

Neither horse seemed distressed, and they both cooled out well. Meanwhile, the great crowd had completely plugged the track, and it took some time to clear a space for the horses to return for the second heat.

The first mile was a back-and-forth battle, with first one and then the other surging ahead, and the mob was more hysterical, and louder, than ever. The second mile was again a series of "desperate rushes," with Fashion leading at the end of it by two or three lengths. Then Gil Patrick held Boston in for a few hundred yards to get his wind and halfway through the third mile, down a slight grade, made another frantic effort to pass the mare. This time Boston finally "took the track," getting fairly ahead of Fashion for the first time in the heat. Our unidentified witness wrote:

The scene which ensued we have no words to describe. Such cheering, such betting, and so many long faces were never seen nor heard before.

After being compelled to give up the track, Joe Laird, with utmost prudence and good sense, took his mare in hand, and gave her time to recover her wind. This run took the shine out of Boston. Instead of pulling him steadily and refreshing him with a slight respite, Gil Patrick kept him at his work after he took the track, and ran this third mile in 1:51½. The pace was tremendous. Nothing short of limbs of steel . . . could stand up under such a press.

On the first turn after passing the stand, Fashion, now fresh again, rallied, and as Boston had not another run in him she cut him down in her stride opposite the quarter-mile post, and the thing was out. The race, so far as Boston was concerned, was past praying for. If anything can parallel Fashion's turn of speed, it is her invincible gameness. She now gradually dropped him, and without further effort on his part . . . she came home a gallant winner in 7:45. Boston pulled up . . . and walked in.

As Joe Laird rode Fashion back to the stands the shouts were so deafening that, had not the president of the club and another gentleman held her bridle she would have not only "enlarged the circle of her acquaintances" very speedily, but "made a mash" of some dozen of the "rank and file" then and there assembled. She looked as if another heat would not "set her back" any.

Another heat, of course, was not necessary. As one of the

judges remarked, "Boston has beaten himself, and Fashion has beaten Boston!" Napoleon, although he had met his Waterloo in this splendid young mare, could console himself with the fact that she had had to set a new American track record to accomplish the feat, and "Old White-Nose" had in no way disgraced himself.

Boston wasn't finished yet. He went back to the stud farm where he "left a heritage of blood which is still a compelling and conquering line upon the American turf." Two of his sons would soon be making racing history, and one in particular, Lexington, would be perhaps the greatest sire the American Thoroughbred has ever known.

13

The Battles
of Boston's Sons

LEXINGTON, by Boston out of Alice Carneal, was foaled in 1850 in Lexington, Kentucky, shortly after Boston died. A worthier heir to the crown has never existed.

His first owner, Dr. Elisha Warfield, called his colt "Darley," and he wanted to race him, but at 72 years of age he felt he was too old to do a good enough job of training. Thus, an odd story unfolds. It seems that Dr. Warfield leased the colt for racing purposes to an ex-slave known only as "Mr. Burbridge's Harry." Harry, who had recently bought his freedom with money earned as a horse trainer, took the colt in hand.

When Darley, a beautiful blood bay, had just turned three, Harry entered him in the Association Stakes at Lexington, one-mile heats. The entry fee was $100, of which Harry and Dr. Warfield each paid half. Darley won in the first two heats, distancing most of the field.

A few days later, still wearing Dr. Warfield's colors and still called Darley, the bay colt entered another race at Lexington. Harry was in a bind. Dr. Warfield, his "partner," had not yet paid Harry his half of the purse from the first race. Moreover, he had not yet come up with his half of the entry fee for the second one. The former slave, determined to run the colt, borrowed the entry fee and courageously told Dr. Warfield that this time he "didn't know nothing about no halves." Darley lost the first heat but came back to win the next two and the race, again distancing most of the field. A famous New Orleans sportsman of the day, Richard Ten Broeck, immediately bought "the Boston colt" and named him Lexington, after his birthplace.

Mr. Ten Broeck evidently bought the colt either before or during this second race (between heats), and he claimed that since he was the owner of the winner he should get half the $1,300 prize. Harry, who had put up the entire entry fee, again bravely stood by his guns and refused. The new owner and his partners, three prominent Kentucky horsemen, gave up on Harry then and tried to tell old Dr. Warfield that half the amount of the purse should be deducted from the purchase price, which was in any event only $2,500, for "the greatest horse in America." But Dr. Warfield was just as stubborn as Harry. For $2,500, he sold Lexington to these men, along with a certified pedigree and a quaint statement that read, "The colt was bred by me, as was also his dam, which I now, and will ever, own . . . ."

Ten Broeck's life history—what's known of it—and his general character and personality at once remind one of Eclipse's O'Kelly. Born in Albany to a "good family," he resigned (some say just before he was expelled) from West Point, then apparently spent ten years or so on Mississippi riverboats. By 1844, he had established himself as quite a figure on the New Orleans racing scene, which was then a racing capital. Somehow, he had made friends with many important turfmen, among them Napoleon Johnson, who had done some training for him. Then he became a power himself—he managed some racetracks in the delta area, and owned part interest in the famous Metairie Course in New Orleans, which was where he planned to take his new horse, Lexington, in 1853.

Considering the great rivalry between the Deep South and Kentucky (this was only fourteen years after the bitterly fought Wagner-Gray Eagle races), we might expect Kentuckians to have been angered at old Dr. Warfield for selling his good colt "down the river." They probably were, in fact, but there were two mitigating circumstances in the sale. First was the "partnership" in the deal of the three Kentucky horsemen, no doubt intended to forestall anger, since Ten Broeck could surely have afforded to pay $2,500 by himself. The second was the upcoming Great State Post Stake, scheduled for the following April 1854, in which Ten Broeck announced Lexington would be entered. (Naming the horse Lexington probably didn't hurt any, either.) The Kentuckians figured that no matter how it was cut, the colt was Kentucky-born and bred and could therefore be considered a representative of their fair state.

The whole country awaited the Great State Post Stake with great anticipation. It was intended, indeed, to be a grand enterprise, and it was hoped by its sponsors that each racing state would send its best horse or horses, thereby settling once and for all which state was supreme. The entry fee was a whopping $5,000, but every horse that ran and wasn't distanced was to get $1,000 back. The winner would take the rest. It was to be in four-mile heats, a distance at which the young Lexington had never yet been tried.

Ten Broeck at once sent the colt to his trainer in Natchez and except for one match race he couldn't resist (Lexington won), ordered him to be rested up the entire winter.

The Great State Post Stakes wasn't, as it turned out, quite as great as its backers had hoped, in terms of entries—only four—but it surpassed all hopes in terms of excitement. The four entries were:

1. Representing Kentucky, LEXINGTON, bay colt, 3 years old, ridden by Henry Meichon at 86 pounds.

2. Representing Mississippi, LECOMPTE, chestnut colt, 3 years old, ridden by "John" at 86 pounds.

3. Representing Alabama, HIGHLANDER, chestnut colt, 4 years old, ridden by Gil Patrick at 100 pounds.

4. Representing Louisiana, ARROW, chestnut gelding, 4 years old, ridden by "Abe" at 97 pounds.

Actually, Kentucky was very well represented in this race, as all of the entries except Highlander had been bred there. And all of the Kentucky-bred entries were sired by "Old White-Nose," the great Boston.

Lexington, as young as he was, was already the acknowledged "best horse" up North in Kentucky. And Lecompte, a chestnut, also three years old, was undefeated. These two colts were considered, in their respective sections of the country, unbeatable. So as a contest among the states, the Great State Post Stakes was something of a bust, but as a duel between Boston's two best sons it was a memorable occasion.

Although the day was fine, it had rained previously, and the track was wet and heavy. Lexington had won three of his four victories in the mud—the only time he had run on a dry track was the only time he had failed to win—so the condition of the course suited him. And when he won the Great State Post Stakes in two heats, the Southern reaction was not that he was a faster horse than their Lecompte but that Lexington simply was a good mudder, nothing more than that. They couldn't wait for Lecompte to get a chance at Lexington on a fast track. The chance would come along almost at once, the very next Saturday, April 8, 1854—a Jockey Club purse for $2,000 at the same track.

It was then that Ten Broeck and his Kentucky partners broke up. The Kentucky contingent, being primarily horse-men, ordered Lexington's shoes pulled for a rest period. Ten Broeck, being primarily a track owner and bettor, couldn't see passing up the Jockey Club purse on Saturday (and the big gate receipts), and he ordered the colt reshod and kept in training. The Kentuckians argued that after his trip down from Kentucky and his recent hard race, another four-mile heat race would be too hard on a mere three-year-old. The upshot of the disagreement was that Ten Broeck bought out his partners and entered Lexington in the race.

Interest was higher than ever. All were hoping for a fast track. Lexington's friends knew, from workouts, that he was not just a good mudder and were anxious for him to prove it, and the Southerners definitely were confident that Lecompte could "walk all over him" on a dry track. The betting was fierce—on both horses and on the time. Actually, there were three horses in the race, as required by the rules, but the third received no attention. His name was Reube, one of those good horses overshadowed by giants.

Our account of this historical race comes from a New Orleans newspaper, the *Times-Democrat*:

The drum taps and the horses dash off with a rush for the first heat, and on passing the first turn Lecompte leads, Lexington being second, and Reube trailing behind . . . Their positions did not vary for nearly three miles, although the pace increased . . . Lexington several times making a brush to take the lead, but Lecompte increasing his speed to prevent it. On entering the fourth mile . . . Lexington partially closed the gap that Lecompte had opened on him, and attempted to outfoot him. The attempt was immense . . . but it was ineffectual.

The spur was freely used to induce him to do what his friends claimed for him—that he was the fastest horse in the world at a brush; but Lecompte baffled all his efforts, kept the lead, and won the heat, amid deafening shouts, by six lengths, in much the quickest time ever made in the world—7:26!

Seven minutes and twenty-six seconds! No wonder the crowd erupted again when the time was announced. This certainly proved that the two colts had not been overestimated *and* that Lexington did not need mud to run on.

Our newspaper account continues:

Lexington soon after the heat appeared much distressed, but he recovered during the recess. Lecompte . . . not having been spurred during the heat, was but little distressed, considering the great time and the heat of the day.

The betting was changed about immediately . . . and Lecompte was the favorite at one hundred to forty against the field.

Each horse came up for the second heat with crest erect, and . . . determined, apparently, to win or die. Lexington this time led the way . . . for nearly two miles by about two lengths, when on coming down the stretch and passing the stands to enter on the third mile, Lecompte, who had been bottled up, commenced his great brush, overhauled Lexington, and passed him.

Both now did their best, and the third mile was a constant strife throughout for the lead, and the quickest in the race, being run in 1:46, but Lecompte, although pushed so hard, never wavered, but ran evenly and steadily along about two lengths ahead.

On the first turn of the fourth mile, Lexington, who at that point was nearly up to his rival, for a moment gave back and lost his stride; but he at once recovered it and pushed on with vigor, but with evidently great effort. All was of no use, for Lecompte came home a winner by four lengths in the astonishing time of 7:38¾, distancing Reube.

For more than twenty years the race of Eclipse and Henry over the Union Course, Long Island, on May 27, 1823, was the quickest on record. . . . In Fashion's race with Boston . . . 1842, the time was 7:32½.

And so a new era began. Lexington had lost to Lecompte this time, but he set things right the following spring by coming back to race against the clock. Ten Broeck rashly boasted that Lexington could actually beat that incredible 7:26 record, and he set out to prove it. Gil Patrick, America's premier jockey, would ride Lexington in the great trial at New Orleans, and Lexington would demonstrate again the coming of age of the American Thoroughbred.

Although racing against time, in order to give him encouragement he would be paced by other horses, taking turns, and he was to get a running start. The track that day was hard as flint, much too hard for comfort and safety.

The pace horses turned out to be of little help to Lexington since, as the *Times-Democrat* remarked about one of them, "at no time was he near enough for Lexington to hear the sound of his hooves," so he might as well have been running alone. And the track was so hard that "Lexington lost his fore plate and half the right hind one, and Gil Patrick, the last mile . . . had no little difficulty keeping him on his course, Lexington making violent efforts to swerve to the right, where it was soft and heavy."

But—with no competition for incentive and with hurting feet and about half his shoes on—Lexington did it. He made good his owner's reckless boast, for his official time for the four miles was a blistering 7:19¾!

The American turf was agog with this new record, and the Lecompte backers were more eager than ever to have another go at Lexington. Ten Broeck was not afraid of Lecompte, and both horses were entered in another Jockey

Club purse at Metairie, New Orleans. This was to be Lexington's greatest challenge, the race that would decide for all time which of Boston's best sons would wear his father's crown.

Again the newspaper account:

When the blankets were stripped from the horses and their magnificent combinations of blood, heart, and muscle stood glistening and flickering in the sun, the crowd . . . could not resist a burst of admiration, at which Lecompte stepped coquetishly about, showing his beautiful chest and branching muscle, while the darker Lexington, with a sedate and intelligent aspect, looked calmly around, as if he felt that the sensation was quite what he expected and deserved.

At length the tap of the drum came, and instantly it struck, the stationary steeds leaped forward with a start that sent everybody's heart into his mouth. With bound on bound, as if life were staked on every leap, they flew up the quarter-stretch, Lexington at the turn drawing his nose a shadow in advance, but when they reached the half-mile post—53 seconds—both were exactly side by side. On they went at the same flying pace, Lexington again drawing gradually forward . . . and increasing up the straight side amid a wild roar of cheers, flew by the stand at the end of the first mile, three-quarters of a length in the lead . . . Time, 1:49½.

Onward they plunge; onward without pause! . . . "By heaven, Lecompte is overhauling him!"

And so he was, for on entering the back-stretch of the second mile the hero of 7:26 made his most desperate effort, reaching first the girth, then the shoulder, then the neck of Lexington, and finally, when he reached the half-mile post, laid himself alongside him, nose by nose . . .

But this equality was only for a moment's term. Lexington threw his eye jealously askant; Gil Patrick relaxed a little of his rein . . . and without a violent or startling effort, the racer of racers stole ahead, gently, but steadily and surely, as before, until he drew himself a clear length in the lead, in which position they closed the second mile. Time, 1:51.

Again the hurrah arises as they pass the stand . . . and swells in still wider volume when Lexington increases his one length to three, from the stand to the turn of the back-stretch. In vain Lecompte struggled; in vain his rider struck him with the steel; his great spirit was a sharper spur, and when his tail fell, as it did from this time out, I could imagine he felt a sinking of the heart as he saw streaming before him the waving flag of Lexington, now held straight out in race-horse fashion, and anon nervously flung up, as if it were a plume of triumph.

The three lengths were increased to four, and again the shout arose, as in this relative condition they went for the third time over the course. Time, 1:51.

The last crisis of the strife had now arrived, and Lecompte, if he had any resources left, must call upon them straight. So thought his rider, for the steel went into his sides, but it was in vain, for he had done his best; while, as for Lexington, it seemed as if he had just begun to run. Gil Patrick now gave him a full rein . . . and it actually seemed as if he were running for the very fun of the thing . . . He had the laurel in his teeth and was going for the distance.

But at this inglorious prospect [of being distanced], Lecompte desperately rallied, and escaped the humiliation by drawing himself a few lengths within the distance pole, while Lexington dashed past the stand, hard in hand, and actually running away with his rider—making the last mile in 1:52¼, and completing the four in the unprecedented time of 7:23¾. I say unprecedented because it beats Lecompte's 7:26, and is therefore the fastest heat that was ever made in a match.

It was also the last as well as the first heat in this race. Lecompte was so utterly done in that he was withdrawn, and Lexington "walked over" to claim the purse.

This was Lexington's last race, too. He returned at last to Kentucky, to the stud. His journey up the river was one of unparalleled glee. As Mr. Trevathan wrote in 1905, "There are still aged gentlemen living in the South who refer to the time 'when we came back from New Orleans with a boatload of money.'"

But Lexington's story—and his greatest glory—had only begun.

14

The Lexington Era

THE GLITTERING chain of great American sires, each link as powerful and vital as the others, continued unbroken. *Diomed, Sir Archy, Timoleon, Boston, and now Lexington, perhaps the greatest of them all.

There were many other important sires during this long period, of course, but the *Diomed line far outshone the others both in terms of quantity and of quality. *Glencoe, for instance, an English import, had a strong influence on the American Thoroughbred, but chiefly through the crossing of his daughters with Lexington or Lexington's sons.

So Lexington was retired after only seven races and only three years on the track. His record—six wins and one loss—is not remarkable on the face of it, but his manner of winning and his record-setting times certainly are. He also won $56,000 during this scanty career, which in those days was an enormous amount. And what with all the betting, his owner, Ten Broeck, made a fortune on the horse.

And here we run across another fascinating mystery. Accounts gleaned from the time conflict, and those written later conflict even more. It is a fact that by the time he retired, or shortly afterward, Lexington was a totally blind horse. Basically, there are two versions of this tragedy.

One version has it that the blood bay stallion had been going blind for some time and that, in fact, in his last race with Lecompte in 1855 he was already sightless. If this is true, of course, Lexington's last victory becomes even more glorious.

It seems unlikely, however. Racehorse owners can be a very secretive, close-mouthed lot, but a totally blind racehorse would be hard to keep secret. Besides, as Mr. Trevathan pointed out in 1905, only ten years before that date old Mr. Ten Broeck still insisted that at the time of Lexington's last race he intended to take the horse to England to challenge that country's horses. In fact, when Lexington was sent up to Harper's farm in Kentucky after the race, he was at first kept in training, which certainly *sounds* as though Ten Broeck planned to continue racing him. He was, after all, only a five-year-old and otherwise perfectly sound.

Therefore, the other version seems more reasonable. That somehow Lexington became more or less *suddenly* blind while he was at Harper's Kentucky farm. There is a story that a drunken groom filled his grain box too full, causing severe colic and then blindness. Another story says he got loose from his stall and gorged himself in a cornfield, unknown to his handlers, just before a hard workout. Both of these particular stories are a little hard to take—unless his handlers were unusually obtuse. Lexington might well have gotten colicky in either of these ways, but a colicky horse ordinarily shows very noticeable symptoms of distress and would not as a rule be given a hard workout.

Still, again, it does seem more likely that Lexington was not blind until after being sent back to Kentucky, but to his death Ten Broeck would never say exactly what happened, if he knew, and now probably no one will ever know.

In any case, the great Lexington did somehow lose his sight at this early age and lived the rest of his long, valuable life in darkness.

At the time of the tragedy, early in 1855, Mr. Ten Broeck was in England setting up some races for Lexington over there. One of his greatest desires was to show up those English horses, and he was sure that Lexington could do it. But not, of course, stone-blind. The news, when it reached Ten Broeck, must have crushed him.

Another famous American sportsman happened to be in England at the same time, however, and Lexington's life story took a happy turn, for a better buyer for the horse could not have been found. He was R. A. Alexander, the aristocratic owner of Woodburn Stud in Kentucky and a fine gentleman, sportsman, and serious student of blood-lines. At this propitious moment, he was in England seeking a suitable stallion to add to his Thoroughbred breeding program. So it was that Lexington, as American a horse as ever lived, changed hands in England for the then-fabulous price of $15,000.

It was still a bargain. Mr. Trevathan tells us:

The name of Lexington was handled with scarcely less deference than that of the Deity. All over the sunny South went the word "Lexington." Far up into the North, even into parts where the race-horse was not known, travelled the word "Lexington." There came a day when any little child of America could have told you the story of Lexington. And the time is not yet past when that name is synonymous with everything that is greatest in a horse. Lexington belonged not alone to the turfmen. He was the heritage of the nation. He was *Lexington* in the minds of the people, and after him there were merely other horses.

This great stallion, called "the Blind Hero of Woodburn," lived out the remainder of his twenty-seven years at Woodburn Stud, with only one little trip away from home. About 1865, in the ferocious days of the Civil War, Lexington and all the breeding stock at Woodburn were threatened by raiders.

The Civil War, naturally, was waged mainly by horse-power and mule power, and the statistics are grim. Robert West Howard, in *The Horse in America*, reports that twice as many horses and mules died as did humans, and that Union commanders claimed a loss of about five hundred horses and mules killed or wounded *every day* by gunshot. Disease took an even worse toll, as epidemics of a "virus plague," pneumonia, influenza, and glanders swept through the army animals of both sides.

Thus it happened that the great stud farms soon became prime targets for raiders. Replacement horses were desperately and constantly needed, and even such a horse as the beloved aging Lexington was not safe. In fact, Woodburn, with its magnificent animals, was the greatest prize of all.

At some time during that terrible war (given dates conflict), Mr. Alexander received a report that an order had gone out to Confederate raiders to capture every horse at Woodburn. If this order had been carried out, the effect on American Thoroughbred breeding would have been catastrophic. But, forewarned, Mr. Alexander arranged a historic and dramatic evacuation.

By night, protected by Alexander's faithful and armed stable men, the entire horse herd of Woodburn, including

Lexington, was secretly led along back roads to the Ohio River. There they were loaded aboard a small fleet of barges and rafts and were safely floated across to Illinois. They remained there, in Union country, and somehow escaped being confiscated until the war was all but over, when they were all returned to Woodburn. This is probably the closest call that a vital Thoroughbred line had experienced since Eclipse's narrow escapes.

This is not a history book, so we won't go into the Civil War except to note the obvious fact that it thoroughly devastated the South as a horse-breeding center. All the great Southern stud farms were destroyed; over a million horses were killed. Other horses survived but were "lost." A captured Thoroughbred, ending the war hundreds of miles from home with no "papers," was to all intents and purposes lost, since its identity could not be proved. Breeding records and pedigrees were burned and scattered. With bred and blood horses wandering back to the blue-grass country after the war, much of the breed's authenticity was lost, too, and many unscrupulous people took the opportunity to invent pedigrees and forge papers during this time of utter chaos.

But with all this, Lexington, at Woodburn again, was meanwhile establishing a line that would be more than ready for racing when the country was.

Lexington's impact on the racing stock of America cannot be overemphasized. During his years at stud he sired over six hundred horses, and nearly every one of them was a good racehorse. It was said at the time that a person could buy any three colts or fillies sired by Lexington and be sure of at least one winner—a fantastic statement but probably true. Yet he sired no great sires. In that respect the chain was broken.

For sixteen years—still a record—Lexington was America's premier sire. His sons and daughters, if they lost a race, quite likely lost it to another of his sons or daughters. As racehorses, his get were unequaled. But now the male line of Lexington is all but extinct.

This great loss is usually blamed on the stupidity of American breeders, who neglected the Lexington line in later years. It is more reasonably explained by the fact that Lexington was purely and simply what is known as a "brood-mare sire." This is a strange, unexplainable quirk of horse breeding, that occasionally there is a truly great horse like Lexington that never "sires sires." His sons were excellent racers, but no more than fair in the stud. Some genetic kink prevented them from passing along their own good qualities to their offspring.

As a brood-mare sire, though, Lexington has never been surpassed. Many another famous stallion of the day and later years got its reputation by being bred to Lexington's daughters. These mares almost without exception inherited Lexington's calm, kindly disposition, which made them motherly, and they were all "good milkers," so that their foals got a good start in life. But there was more to it than that. That same genetic quirk that, sadly, nearly ended the male line's influence also brought about the fact that a breeder could mate a Lexington mare with almost *any* stallion and come up with a winner. These mares were almost unbelievable.

But Lexington's sons were far from failures on the racetracks. In just one year he sired the three most famous racehorses of their day: Asteroid, Kentucky, and Norfolk. These three horses were valued then at about $50,000 apiece, which by today's standards would easily make them million-dollar horses. All three were out of daughters of *Glencoe, another brood-mare sire.

That these three horses could attract so much attention

and stir up so much violent controversy at that time—at the end of the Civil War—says quite a lot about them and about the American racing public. It seems incredible that people would even think about horse racing, yet it was said that in 1864 and the years immediately following, the sometimes bitter argument over the relative merits of the three horses was "daily in the mouths of thousands." Or perhaps it is not so strange. It is also said that horse racing, and these three horses in particular, had a great deal to do with helping to heal the awful wounds of the war. As Mr. Trevathan expressed it, "The people were sick of war . . . and they turned to the turf with eagerness. *It was the only practical means of reunion at the time. . . .* Where the horses ran, there the men from the South and the men from the North met to exchange cordial greeting."

If a race ever had been arranged among the three sons, there's no question but that, Civil War or no, the attendance would have topped anything yet seen because such a race was the fond dream of every racing fan in America. It was not to be, however. Only once did even two of them—both three-year-olds—meet.

Kentucky, changing hands from one wealthy New Yorker to another, finally winding up belonging to August Belmont, remained in the East where he was unconquerable. Asteroid, owned by his breeder, Mr. Alexander, was the Kentucky champion. In September 1866, New York became much excited as word reached there that Asteroid was on his way from Woodburn to New York to meet at last his half-brother, Kentucky. As we say, war or no war, such was the fever engendered by this promised meeting that people poured into New York by the trainloads, even coming from as far away as Texas. Out at Jerome Park where the race was to be held, a crowd of hundreds gathered to watch the two horses work out every morning. Then, suddenly, disaster struck. In a morning trial, in the mud, Asteroid "sprung a tendon," and his racing career was ended—as were, of course, all hopes for settling the great controversy. Mr. Alexander took the lame horse home to Woodburn amid great general sadness and disappointment.

Meanwhile, the other one of this particular big three, Norfolk, had gone all the way out to California, so that part of the argument would never be resolved, either. It was only a few years later, however, in the 1870s, that the cross-continental trains did begin to bring Kentucky and New York horses West to answer the boasts of Californians.

California had, by then, a good start toward what was to become its extensive Thoroughbred industry, and the state was about the last stronghold of the four-mile heat race. For it was during this period, "the Lexington era," that the day of the four-miler began to wane, and the Eastern tracks were tending toward shorter races.

The last of the really national four-mile heat races was held in California in 1873 at Ocean View Park. The big race was held for two reasons: to give horse racing a needed boost in California by creating a great deal of interest; and because Californians (that old "sectional rivalry" again) felt that they had, in a horse called Thad Stevens, the best four-miler going, and they were eager to show Kentucky what their home-bred could do.

Both these objectives were accomplished by setting the purse at an astounding $20,000. This tempting prize created interest, and it also made the long, tedious trip West seem worth the effort to the owners of four of the East's best distance horses: True Blue, Joe Daniels, Hubbard, and Mamie Hall. (True Blue was sired by Lexington, Mamie Hall by Norfolk.) Hubbard went lame in training and was withdrawn, leaving three Easterners to accept Thad Stevens' challenge. The Californians naturally put their money on "Old Thad," while the Easterners' favorite was Joe Daniels. True Blue was also highly thought of in the betting, but he arrived in California only a short time before the race, and many felt that he would not have enough time to recover fully from the long train ride.

The race began grimly for the Golden State. Joe Daniels won the first heat, followed by True Blue. Old Thad was fifty yards back. In the second heat it was again Joe Daniels' and True Blue's fight all the way, this time with True Blue coming in ahead. Thad Stevens, to the Californians' dismay, was eight lengths behind the others. It began to look as though a great deal of California's gold would be leaving the state that day, and the crowd was tense.

The third heat was a stunner to almost everyone concerned. As before, Joe Daniels and True Blue (who appeared leg-weary) took the lead. But soon Old Thad, for whom it was now or never, made his play, and before the first mile was up, he had passed them both. The two Eastern jockeys, eying each other, closed up on Thad momentarily, one on each side, but he pulled ahead of them again and kept his lead of about three lengths throughout the third mile. At that point Joe Daniels passed True Blue and "made play for the Pacific-sloper." Just then, True Blue faltered and was stopped, lame. Thad Stevens was now about six lengths ahead of Joe Daniels, and even though the Eastern horse gave it all he had, he could not close the gap. Thad won the third heat in 7:67. The fourth heat was a tremendous triumph for the Californians. Old Thad led all the way and "won in a big gallop by ten lengths" as the crowd went mad with joy and surged onto the track to congratulate the old horse.

There were many other great races during this post-Civil War period, some of them at the four-mile distance. Lexington's old record of 7:19¾ was not broken, however, until 1874, about twenty years later. It was broken by Fellowcraft, who was out of one of Lexington's splendid daughters, and he lowered the record by one-quarter of a second.

In general, by the time "the Blind Hero of Woodburn" died in 1876, a new kind of Thoroughbred had emerged on the American scene—the "cup horse," bred and trained for a different kind of race. This "new breed" was no longer asked to run three or more four-mile heats in one afternoon. Instead, it was expected to get away from the post fast and run like blazes for a mile or two in just one heat. The four-milers hung on hard—in 1876, a horse named Ten Broeck lowered the record to 7:15¾—but the day of the sprinter was approaching fast.

Omaha (by Gallant Fox), Triple Crown Winner, 1935. *Wide World Photos.*

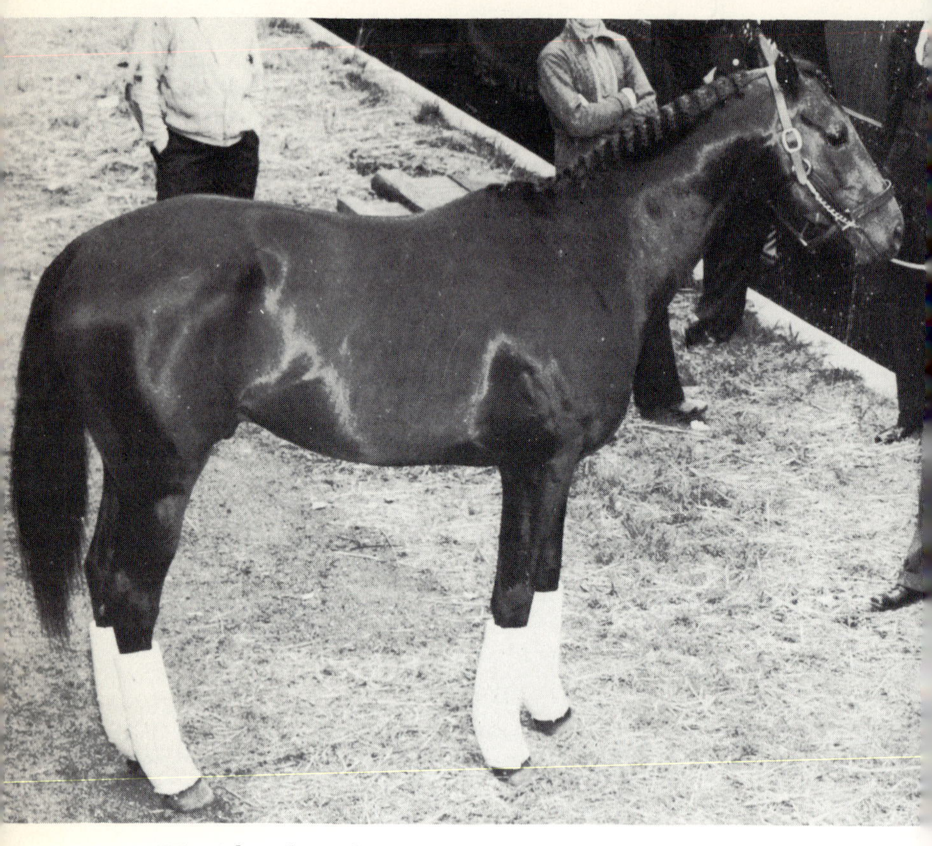

War Admiral, Triple Crown Winner, 1937. *Wide World Photos.*

(On facing page) Whirlaway, Triple Crown Winner, 1941. *Wide World Photos.*

Count Fleet, Triple Crown Winner, 1943. *Wide World Photos.*

Secretariat, Triple Crown Winner, 1973. *Wide World Photos.*

(On facing page above) Citation, Triple Crown Winner, 1948. *Wide World Photos.*

(On facing page below) Assault, Triple Crown Winner, 1946. *Wide World Photos.*

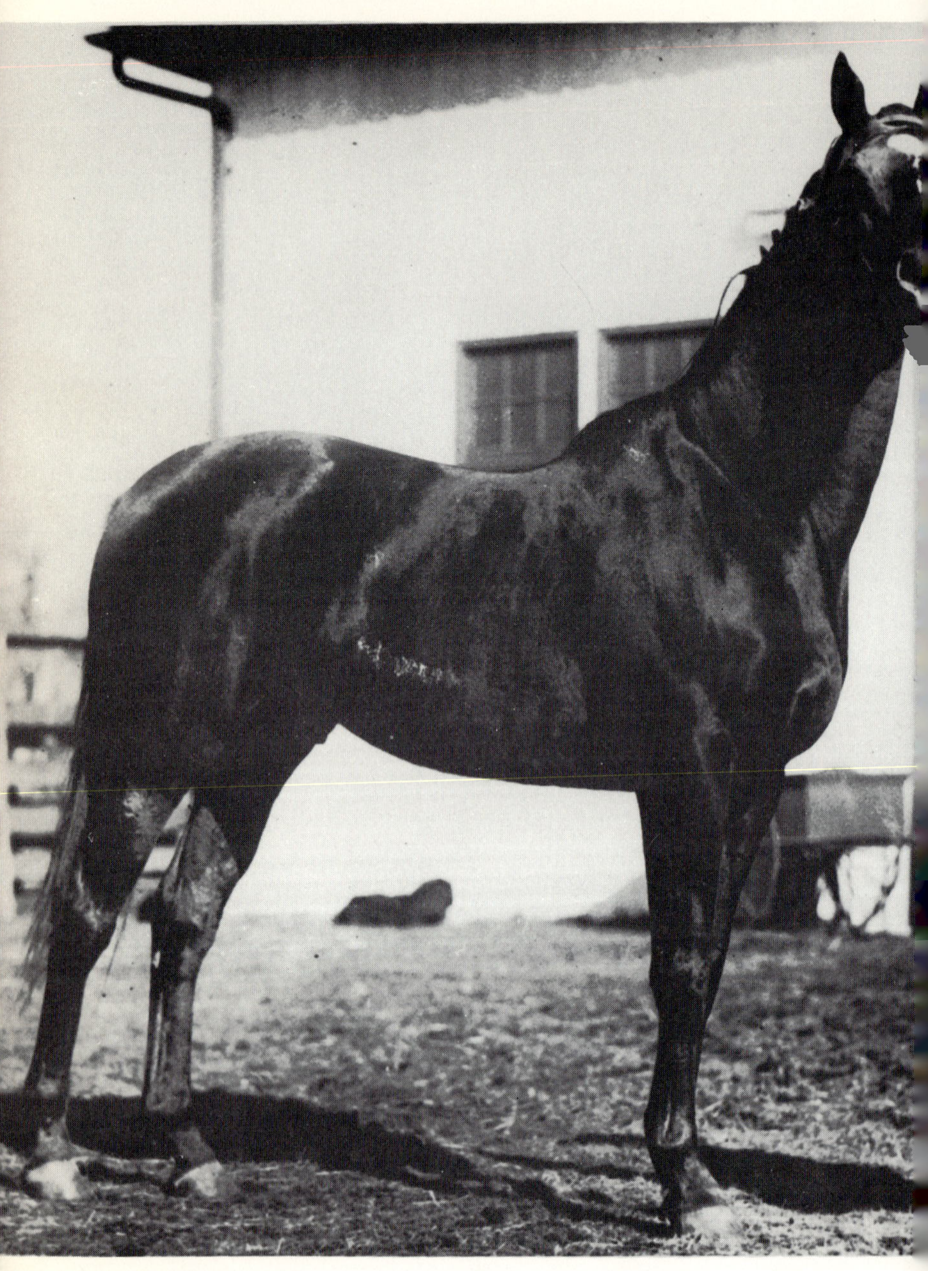

Man o' War, one of the greatest racehorses of all time, 1924. *Wide World Photos.*

15

Between Wars

LEXINGTON, while the most powerful force in American Thoroughbred breeding for a long time, was not solely responsible for its great progress. One of his best helpers was the English import *Glencoe, foaled in 1831. After a good racing career and a good start on a stud career in England, he was shipped to America in 1837. Like Lexington, he was primarily a brood-mare sire, and his daughters helped make Lexington's reputation the same way Lexington's own daughters would later make other stallions famous. Lecompte, Asteroid, Kentucky, and Norfolk all came from *Glencoe's daughters, as did a great many more fine racehorses and breeding stock.

Another famous sire of the post-Civil War period was *Bonnie Scotland, who almost went unnoticed. Imported from England to Boston, Massachusetts, he was then resold and taken to Ohio. There he lived in virtual seclusion and certainly without any fame, for there were almost no Thoroughbred mares in Ohio at that time. After changing hands a few times, however, he finally got his chance in 1872 when he was bought by a real Thoroughbred breeder, given good mares (many of them Lexington mares), and started turning out a line of successful racehorses that the public called "the Busy Bs."

While American breeders were furnishing horses like Longfellow, Hanover, Domino, and Ben Brush, other Americans were building racetracks for them to prove themselves on, and yet other Americans were going to the new tracks to watch them.

Between the end of the Civil War and the end of the century, horse racing enjoyed enthusiastic popularity. This was indeed a very busy period for the American turf. Races were getting shorter, following the style in England, and therefore younger horses could be raced and more races could be watched each afternoon. The American turf scene was, in short, approaching what it is today.

Most of the great annual races were run for the first time in this half-century. Among these classics were the three races for three-year-olds that today make up the American Triple Crown. The first was the Belmont Stakes, which was actually run as early as 1867, although at other New York tracks until the new Belmont track opened in 1905. (Both the race and the track were named after August Belmont, a leading New York turf figure.) The second jewel of the Crown to be inaugurated was the Preakness, in 1873, then and always run at Pimlico in Maryland. The last, and most famous, was the Kentucky Derby at Churchill Downs, Louisville, Kentucky, the first running of which was in 1875.

There is a strange aspect of this first Kentucky Derby that sooner or later catches the researcher's attention. The winner of the 1875 Derby was Aristides, called by some writers a "little no-account horse." That a little no-account horse should win the first Kentucky Derby does, of course, make a good story. But subsequent research turns up the information that Aristides was sired by *Leamington, a famous stallion, and was out of Sarong, one of those great Lexington mares. By breeding, then, Aristides was hardly "no-account." Nor was he "no-account" by performance, since in 1875 he not only won the first Derby but was also the top money winner for that year. All of which makes a little suspect the often-told story of how little Aristides, highly outclassed, won the first Derby against all odds.

In its hundred-year history, however, the Kentucky Derby has had more than its share of surprise winners. Again and again, a horse has won the Derby that "shouldn't have," that barely ever won another race in its life. Such is the prestige of the Derby that although the purses have sometimes been quite low, it is the dream of most horse owners and jockeys to win at least one. The usually large and crowded field may account for some of the surprises.

The first jockey to ride three Derby winners was Isaac Murphy, who was also the first jockey to enter racing's Hall of Fame. He was black, born into slavery in 1860, and the greatest jockey of his time, highly courageous and capable of handling any racehorse. Perhaps his most outstanding characteristic, in a time when racehorses were often whipped and spurred mercilessly, was Murphy's refusal to use either means of "encouragement."

In spite of the fact that "the wrong horse" has often won the Kentucky Derby, and some of our best horses have not (Man o' War, for instance, was never entered), some have gone on to be truly great. In all these years only nine three-year-olds have managed to win and wear the Triple Crown, and they have all been outstanding horses:

1919—Sir Barton
1930—Gallant Fox

    1935—Omaha (by Gallant Fox)
    1937—War Admiral
    1941—Whirlaway
    1943—Count Fleet
    1946—Assault
    1948—Citation
    1973—Secretariat

And it was Churchill Downs' famous manager and promoter of the Derby, Colonel Matt Winn, who may well have saved racing in America from total extinction.

So vastly popular had racing come to be during the period following the Civil War, so large had the purses grown, and so heavy the wagering with the bookmakers, that as the end of the century approached, racing nearly "boomed" itself right out of business. Attracted by all the money to be had, the wrong people gradually got control, and eventually all the doping, fixing, and general finagling got so bad that the public's reaction was revulsion. Racing, after its rapid expansion, acquired a very bad name for itself.

Two things saved it: the parimutuel system, and, as before in England, the high-minded, wealthy sportsmen.

The parimutuel system, a crude prototype of today's elaborate electronic gear, had been tried before but had failed to become popular with the public. The public preferred its bookies even though many of them were crooked. By 1908, however, the smell had got so bad that bookmakers were outlawed—as even racing itself was being outlawed in more and more places. So Colonel Winn, to save that year's Derby, brought out and set up the old parimutuel betting machinery. This time it worked. There were no bookmakers to compete with it, and the public accepted it.

Even so, in 1910, New York State outlawed racing,

following the example of many other states. The grand new Belmont Park and all the rest were closed. Since New York was considered the capital of racing in this country, it was felt that this meant the end of the American turf, even with the new betting system.

It was then that people like Belmont, Whitney, and Vanderbilt stepped in. The American Stud Book had been established in 1868. To this was now added the Jockey Club, and later the Thoroughbred Racing Association. With the authority of these institutions behind them, the great sportsmen of the day ruthlessly cleaned up racing to the point where the states—and the public—could once again approve of and enjoy it. Nowadays, of course, racing is probably the most carefully policed sport in the world, which it must be to succeed.

There were many great horses during this time, too, which also helped to keep the sport alive. One of the fans' favorite racehorses, a homely, "built wrong" chestnut gelding named Exterminator, was a descendant of *Messenger. He was foaled just in time to see the gradual rebirth of American racing in 1915, two years before Man o' War was born.

Exterminator was a worker. He ran in a hundred races during his eight years of racing and, amazingly, won fifty of them—under high weights. He was a big horse, nearly seventeen hands high, and extremely rangy and gawky. The adoring public gave him the affectionate names of "Old Bones" and "the Galloping Hatrack." He was also a very gentlemanly horse, extremely biddable and well behaved. Often, when the starter had a bad actor to line up, he would put Exterminator right beside it. Exterminator would then do his part by setting a good example and, if necessary, even leaning against the rough horse to remind it of its manners.

Since Exterminator was five years old and in his prime

during Man o' War's famous three-year-old year, it has always been a rich source of discussion as to which horse was better, for they never raced against each other. That was not the fault of Exterminator's owner, a hot-tempered man named Willis Kilmer. He pestered Man o' War's owner, Mr. Riddle, for a race between the two. But for some reason Mr. Riddle kept avoiding Mr. Kilmer, who kept following him around challenging him. It is impossible to say now why Mr. Riddle did not take up this constant challenge. It would certainly have been one of the great races of the century. Perhaps he simply resented being pestered. In any case they never met, and so the discussions about what might have happened will never end.

As for Man o' War, he was without question the superhorse of the twentieth century, maybe even of *any* century.

16

Man o' War

IF EVER there was a horse that was a "legend in his own time," that horse was Man o' War, the magnificent chestnut stallion. As a racehorse, the only thing that ever beat him was bad racing luck: A horse appropriately named Upset went down in history as the only horse ever to win over Man o' War. This happened when "Big Red" got off to a bad start and later got boxed in until too close to the finish line to make it up. Had there been a few more yards left in the race, he would have won, so strongly was he gaining. To all intents and purposes, then, Man o' War was undefeated. Like so many of the unbeatable horses in the past, Man o' War was a horse of the future, ahead of his time in the evolutionary process. He put all the good horses of his day, horses that otherwise would have become much more famous, in the shade, "eclipsing" them as Eclipse had done so long before.

Man o' War was an ideal example of the superhorse, the very essence of the word "Thoroughbred."

Foaled on August Belmont's Kentucky farm in 1917, Man o' War came from good bloodlines. His dam was Mahubah, a daughter of the imported stallion *Rock Sand. His sire was Fair Play, a son of the notorious Hastings. All three of these horses had reputations for being temperamental, especially Hastings. When Hastings would run, he was a great racehorse, but he was a virtually unmanageable hellion, more interested in trying to kill his jockey and the other horses than in running. His son, Fair Play, was better but still bad-tempered. Man o' War inherited some of this wickedness, and it was one of the things that made him a superhorse.

The subject of temperament in the racehorse is another mystery. Why have so many of the truly great horses been so hard to live with? Eclipse, for instance. It would be easy to say here that this fieriness just goes along with breeding for speed and courage—that "heart" that makes a Thoroughbred want to win. And perhaps this is true. A sluggish horse or a timid one would not, one would think, make an ideal racehorse. Yet there have been many like Lexington and Exterminator, too—as courageous as they come, but kindly and friendly. Brown Jack, a famous and beloved English racehorse, had speed and courage to spare, but he would almost doze off at the post and treat the race as a big frolic, lolloping along playfully until the last possible moment, then winning in an almost chuckling burst of speed. Around the stable he was about as temperamental as an elderly plow horse. It is not enough to say that Brown Jack was so superior to his opponents that he could afford to be relaxed and playful. So were Man o' War and Eclipse and all the other "hell raisers." Some great horses just seem able to confine their aggressiveness to actual competition, while others are always belligerent.

Had he been an ordinary horse, Man o' War would have been called downright mean. But in him this over-aggressiveness came out as arrogance, and it was a big part of what thousands flocked to the track to see. "Big Red" would bound out onto the track practically bellowing a challenge to the world to come and try to beat him. He loved to run. If he hadn't, he could never have been wrestled as far as the starting gate.

It was his trainer, Louis Feustel, who brilliantly handled the red colt and turned his innate warlike character into a competitive desire to run. Perhaps no other trainer could have done it, but Feustel had known and worked with Mahubah, Fair Play, and the infamous Hastings (who regularly went berserk), and he understood this colt. He understood that it would have been hopeless to try to force the big, strong, hardheaded colt to do anything. A fight with Man o' War was a fight lost.

Neither, Feustel realized, could such a horse be coddled into anything with kindness. All of Man o' War's chroniclers describe him as being regal, majestic, aloof, with an "aura of greatness" and "the look of eagles." They seem to have been awed by his very presence. He was not a horse, even as a colt, to be won over by sugar cubes and sweet talk.

Feustel understood all of this, and like John Oakley, Eclipse's jockey, he was just the right person for this kind of horse. His training method can best be summed up in his own words. He "went along" with Man o' War, he said, and would "figure things out with him and let him believe he'd done it for himself." This intelligent philosophy, or psychology, plus some good jockeys with strong arms made Man o' War invincible.

Beyond his aggressive temperament, Man o' War also possessed a body and legs that made him "the perfect racing machine." Like Eclipse, Man o' War was born in a time when shorter-coupled racehorses with close, quick stride were in fashion; and, like Eclipse, Man o' War was unfashionably long, tall and rangy, with a big, high-bounding stride. It was said at first that such a high, loose way of going was a waste of time and motion, but his record-shattering races soon put that theory back on the shelf.

His racing record is well known. He raced twenty-one times as a two- and three-year-old, winning all but the flukey Upset race. The *Daily Racing Form* records, which summarize each race, are full of comments like, "won easily, second and third driving," "won under a stout pull," and "won in a canter." So easily did he win his races that usually as he passed the finish line his jockey was standing up in the stirrups, trying to slow him down, while the rest of the field was struggling mightily far behind. One famous photo shows Man o' War going under the wire "under a stout pull" as the next horse is just thrashing around the turn, a full hundred lengths to the rear!

In other words, Man o' War was so much faster than his opponents that he beat them "in a canter" while they were running their very hearts out. No one will ever know just how fast he was. He never ran the whole distance at top speed. Even so, he broke one record after another. It will always be a source of debate and great curiosity as to what kind of records he could have set had he put some effort into it.

Man o' War could have raced more than those two years. He was never unsound a day in his life. But he was retired at the end of his three-year-old form for the same reasons that Eclipse was retired after only two years. There are few owners who would let their horses be so humiliated for a second or third place, and the handicappers were threatening to put 140 pounds and more on him if he came back.

Man o' War's record in the stud was very creditable—out of 379 offspring, 61 were stakes winners and many more were less important winners—but it wasn't as good a record as it might have been. It is said that, later on in life especially, he was given rather mediocre mares. Nonetheless, he sired many well-known racehorses, and his line is still powerful. Among others, he sired Crusader, Hard Tack (Seabiscuit's sire), War Relic, American Flag, Battleship, and, of course, the Triple Crown winner and Horse of the Year, War Admiral.

Man o' War was retired still a colt, and he lived out his thirty years of life in comfort, dignity, and adulation at Faraway Farm in Kentucky where thousands of visitors came to see "de mostest hoss," as his devoted groom Will Harbut christened him. Man o' War never completely settled down. He was always, even at an advanced age, ready to race the colts in the pasture; he never entirely quit his token battle at being tacked up and exercised; and he never lost any of his great spirit and sense of superiority. A photo of him as a plump but still handsome twenty-seven-year-old shows him rearing high in the air, "playing up."

He died in 1947, about a month after his faithful groom died. The great horse was buried with ceremony at Faraway Farm under an impressive statue of himself, where visitors still come to pay their respects to the most famous American racehorse since Lexington.

The next really beloved racehorse to come along, one that won the hearts of racing fans throughout the country, was Man o' War's grandson, Seabiscuit.

17

The Biscuit
and the Cougar

Seabiscuit, sired by Man o' War's son Hard Tack, had a life story that surpasses anything yet told here in heart-rending warmth and sheer melodrama. His life—as a racehorse, at least—was almost over before he was even three years old.

Foaled at Claiborne Farm in Kentucky in 1932, this greatest grandson of Man o' War immediately "fell on hard times." His first owner nearly raced him right into the ground as a two-year-old with thirty-five races. He won only five of them. The result of such a punishing schedule was that he acquired "popped knees and a case of nerves" and sank to the level of a $2,500 claiming race.

For some reason the runty little bay colt, lame and in disgrace, appealed to a Californian, Charles Howard, and Seabiscuit's luck changed. Howard bought him for $8,000 and turned him over to his trainer, "Silent Tom" Smith. A relationship grew between Tom Smith and the abused colt that was to last the rest of their lives and be a prime force in Seabiscuit's amazing career.

Like Louis Feustel and Man o' War, Tom Smith and Seabiscuit understood each other. The first thing Tom did was give the lame colt what his legs and nerves needed most—rest and reassurance. Seabiscuit would always be more or less lame, but his heart—and Tom Smith's faith— would carry him through. Once when another horseman made the remark that Seabiscuit couldn't even walk right, Silent Tom is said to have replied, "Runs, though." And he surely did that!

In 1937, when Seabiscuit was five years old, Tom brought his newly rested horse to California, and he was entered in the Santa Anita Handicap, a race that, year after year, was to become the main goal of Seabiscuit's life. In his first attempt to win it, he lost to a horse named Rosemont by only a nose, and it was his own fault. Always a lazy horse, he made it his habit to loaf in the stretch if he thought he'd won it, just prick up his ears and "cool it," not working any harder than he had to. That was what he did this time, and he misjudged Rosemont's ability to catch him.

The racing men in California misjudged Seabiscuit, too. They misinterpreted his laziness as simple lameness. How many times Mr. Howard and Tom Smith must have heard the old horseman's saying, "They never come back!" But they were determined that Seabiscuit would disprove the adage. That year he ended the season by winning the San Juan Capistrano by seven lengths and even setting a new track record for the distance. All in all, he won $168,580 racing that year. Not bad for a crippled $8,000 colt.

His nerves had mended, but he was still buck-kneed, as his photos plainly show. Another "cripple," his regular jockey and lifelong friend, Red Pollard, rode Seabiscuit to many wins the following year, too. But when it came time to have another go at the Santa Anita Handicap, Pollard, whose nickname was "the Cougar," was unable to ride. He had a broken collarbone at the moment. (At one time or another, Pollard had broken almost every bone he had.) So while "the Cougar" watched anxiously, another great jockey rode Seabiscuit in the 1938 Santa Anita. This was George Woolf, whose nickname was "the Iceman" because of his cool daring. He needed every bit of it in this race when, coming into the back stretch, Seabiscuit was lying twelfth, eleven horses packed solidly in front of him. In spite of the load he was carrying (140 pounds), somehow Seabiscuit, in the next record-breaking half-mile, managed to get through the mob and take the lead. The California crowd went wild at this astonishing feat. But the weight and that incredible half-mile were just a mite too much for "the Biscuit," and Stagehand, carrying only 100 pounds, caught him on the run to the wire. It was eyeball-to-eyeball the rest of the way, but Seabiscuit lost by a whisker. Once again the Santa Anita jinx had robbed him of the victory he and his friends most craved.

By this time the Easterners had heard of the California wonder, and there was a great demand for Seabiscuit to meet his "uncle," War Admiral. War Admiral was a much more impressive-looking horse than the little Biscuit, and his performances matched his regal looks. In 1937 he had become Horse of the Year and a Triple Crown winner.

A match race was set up at Belmont Park for $100,000. Accordingly, Seabiscuit, along with his mascots—Pumpkin, a palomino pony, and Pocatell, a mongrel dog—were all put into a train and headed East. But Seabiscuit was tired again. His legs had stood up so far but wouldn't take much more, and he was getting ornery. He trained so poorly at Belmont that the race was called off. The Easterners were disappointed, but they could at least consider it a partial victory since it wasn't their horse that had gone lame and quit. Once again Mr. Howard, Tom Smith, and Red Pollard heard, "They don't come back." Seabiscuit, they were assured again, was through.

Nevertheless, after a rest of a month or two, they trooped back to California for the Hollywood Gold Cup. By now the horse was well known and loved—for his sheer courage if nothing else—and Californians knew him affectionately as "the Biscuit," "Pops," and "Old Pappy." And his slow, lame shamble to the post, his calm, dignified bearing, made these elderly-sounding names seem right for him.

A few days later "Pops" showed the youngsters how to run, lame or not, in the Hollywood Gold Cup. Eight lengths behind at the turn heading into the backstretch, Seabiscuit, egged on by his thousands of screaming fans, "turned it on" in a heart-stopping display of speed that brought him home a winner by a length and a half! He had done the impossible again—he had "come back."

And once again Mr. Howard and Sam Riddle, War Admiral's owner, agreed to match their famous horses. This time it was to be at Pimlico in Maryland, a mile and $\frac{3}{16}$, 120 pounds on each horse, for only $15,000. The money wasn't important. Both owners—and the fans on each side—just wanted the question settled.

Seabiscuit and his little troop of mascots once again entrained for the East Coast. It was on November 1, 1938, that War Admiral, a four-year-old, was to meet Seabiscuit, now six and perpetually lame. Was it possible that the little bay with the crooked front legs could beat last year's Triple Crown winner? Charles Howard and Tom Smith and Red Pollard—and Seabiscuit—thought so. The East Coast did not agree, and the money put down on War Admiral that day would have been enough to start a good-sized bank.

Since Pollard was—as so often—out of commission with

more broken bones, George Woolf again rode the Biscuit in this historic meeting. He couldn't have ridden a better race. Much to the surprise and dismay of The Admiral's followers, Woolf took the track immediately and stayed there. War Admiral was not a lazy or timid horse. He hung on like fury, and when they came to the backstretch, he gave it all he had, almost coming neck and neck with little Seabiscuit for a while. But that was *all* he had. Try as he might, the greatest son of Man o' War could not get past the greatest grandson. The little bay just kept pulling away. He won by four lengths—and set a new track record. Afterward, in the winner's circle, so unimpressed was Seabiscuit by his fantastic achievement that he tried to eat his floral wreath. Food first, congratulations later, seemed to be the way he felt about it.

"Old Pappy's" return to California was greeted with an ecstatic welcome. He had certainly put that Eastern horse in its place.

But the crooked front legs won another round in their constant battle with his brave spirit. In February of 1939, three months after his world-famous victory over War Admiral, he was in a race at Santa Anita when he broke down again. Although it happened long before the finish line—everyone could see him suddenly give way—he kept on coming. Immediately past the wire, Woolf stopped him short, got down, and led him back while the stunned, silent crowd watched. The horse could scarcely walk.

Broken down. Surely this time he was finished. Not even Seabiscuit could come back again. His loving fans gave him up and mourned his loss.

But his closest friends did not. In March they took him to the farm to see what they could do for him—Pollard (still unable to ride), Mr. Howard, and the groom, Harry

Bradshaw. Tom Smith had to stay at the track with the other horses.

And it became a single-minded obsession with all of them: Seabiscuit just had to run in one more race—the Santa Anita Handicap—and Pollard, suffering from a broken leg that refused to heal, just *had* to ride him in it.

Seabiscuit himself now presented the three determined men with their worst obstacles. Normally a calm, gentle horse, he became difficult. He had not had a real rest on a farm in so long that he didn't know what to do with himself, and this enforced inactivity galled him. The country life was not for him. He wanted the crowds and the excitement. And he didn't want to rest, he wanted to run. When they finally started working him a little, they had to fight with him constantly to keep him from running and hurting himself. They also had his gluttonous appetite to fight. While he was racing, he could work off his calories and stay slim, but now he had to go on a strict diet so as not to be too fat for the Santa Anita Handicap. Seabiscuit soon lost his genial disposition and became a terrible grouch, spending most of his time squealing and kicking for more food. It was a bad summer.

And everyone, except those directly involved, knew it was hopeless. Seabiscuit would never win the Santa Anita Handicap, and "the Cougar," on crutches, would never ride him in it.

But Seabiscuit and Red Pollard would not give up their dream. Just this one more race—that was all they asked. Pollard's leg by now, after having been rebroken and reset several times, was a fragile mess. One little bump would break it again. But he said wryly, "Old Pops and I have four good legs between us—maybe it'll be enough."

And so, both of them more or less hobbling, they came to

Santa Anita for one last try. Even they knew that they would never get another chance. Only a miracle had made this one possible.

There were 80,000 people at Santa Anita that day, and every one of them wanted desperately, against all good sense, to see the Biscuit and the Cougar win.

It may have been the most dramatic horse race in history. After about three-quarters of a mile, Seabiscuit and Pollard moved up in the field, trying for the rail. When they did, Whichcee's rider, Basil James, known for his tricks and boldness, banged his horse hard against Seabiscuit. The two "cripples" almost fell.

But the Cougar was no tenderfoot, either. They were coming into the stretch for home now, and the angered Pollard got Seabiscuit back in stride, coming up on the outside of James. Then, with so much at stake, with his fragile leg to think about, when perhaps he should have played it safe and steered clear, Pollard began to pull in toward James, forcing him tight to the rail. Even the bold James got scared, and Whichcee quit.

At that point, Mr. Howard's other horse *Kayak II came on strong, but the Biscuit and the Cougar, both in pain by now, held him off, too, and—at last!—they won the Santa Anita Handicap.

Or did they? As soon as James got down off his horse he ran to the stewards claiming "Foul!"

For two endless minutes, two minutes of absolute silence in that jam-packed grandstand, Red Pollard sat quietly on Seabiscuit's back, waiting to hear if he should head for the winner's circle, or if Seabiscuit's old jinx was still working, after all. You could have heard a horse's tail swish.

Then Seabiscuit's win was verified. James's foul claim had been disallowed. They *had* done it! The two cripples, on their "four good legs," had come back again.

Seabiscuit never ran another race, but he didn't have to. He had finally won the only race that mattered. Now he could go back to the farm and eat all he wanted for the rest of his life.

He had earned it. Almost as a sideline in his crazy, courageous career, he had beaten all records to become the top money-winning horse in history. He could buy an awful lot of hay and oats and maybe a carrot now and then, too, with $437,730 in his sock.

18

More New Breeds

EVEN IF IT were possible to write it, a complete history of the Thoroughbred would make a book so large and heavy that no one could lift it, let alone make any sense out of it. But no book that deals with the development of the Thoroughbred, however sketchily, should leave out one extremely important aspect of this development: the mighty contributions of this new breed to other new breeds that followed.

The Thoroughbred must be called an English invention since its origins were British. Although the American colonists were hot on their heels, the American Thoroughbred got its start with English imports. The other new breeds that we'll now discuss briefly are, however, 100 per cent American. True, imported stock of all kinds went into their foundations, but the same can be said of the "native"

English stock, which began with the Phoenicians and continued to rely heavily on imports for centuries.

It was the settlers of the New World that "put it all together" and, as need and desire dictated, produced the Quarter Horse, the American Saddle Horse, the Tennessee Walking Horse, the Standardbred, and the Morgan. All of these except the Morgan—which will be considered later— were heavily influenced by the Thoroughbred.

It would be impossible to put the beginnings of these American breeds in chronological order. As with the Thoroughbred, and any new breed, the very beginnings are nebulous and sometimes only realized afterward. Each of these American breeds deserves a book of its own (and many have been written), and here we'll just try to show how the Thoroughbred influenced each one.

THE QUARTER HORSE

As so often in the history of any breed, we find in the Quarter Horse an outstanding "breeding freak"; in this case, a nearly pony-sized little stallion named *Janus. As it turned out, *Janus was a prophetic name for this mighty mite. It means two-faced, and if ever a horse had two distinct "faces," it was *Janus. Foaled in England in 1746 (two years before Matchem was foaled), he was "of the blood." Although he was only about 14.2 hands, the average size of the English racehorse at that time was only a couple of inches taller.

Imported to Virginia in 1756 as a ten-year-old, *Janus, a winning four-miler of endless endurance and no particular "short speed," soon began to show his two faces. On the one hand, when he was bred to Thoroughbred-type mares, he got endurance horses like himself. His influence on the Thoroughbred breed is often overlooked, but he appears in the earliest pedigrees of many famous racehorses, including Regret, the only filly ever to win the Kentucky Derby, and Exterminator.

On the other hand, when *Janus was bred, as he so often was, to the Virginians' "quarter-pathers"—those little speedsters of mixed bred, Hobbie, and Chicasaw blood—he produced sprinters such as had never been seen before.

*Janus' outstanding conformation trait was his tremendously powerful hindquarters, and this trait he passed on to all his get. It was said that a " *Janus horse" could be recognized instantly by its heavy, muscular quarters. And *Janus horses soon abounded in the South. Rarely, if ever, has there been a more popular sire. The Virginians farther North had lost interest in quarter racing soon after *Janus arrived, but when he was shunted southward, he was warmly welcomed. Until he was over thirty years old, he traveled about the southland, standing at farm after farm, and today the extremely numerous and popular tribe of the Quarter Horse still clearly bears his stamp. The modern Quarter Horse, with its heavily developed haunches, is a recognizable *Janus horse, as it was over two hundred years ago.

THE STANDARDBRED

We have already touched on the Standardbred in our discussion of *Messenger, another "two-faced" stallion that produced, on the one hand, great four-mile racehorses like American Eclipse and, on the other, fabulous trotters and pacers, while he himself could neither trot nor pace. On the Standardbred side, then, it is only fair to say that he owed a great deal to the mares—those trotting and pacing descendants of the Irish Hobbie and the Galloway that were then so numerous in the New World.

What might be called the first real Standardbred was foaled in 1849, a brute-ugly, big horse owned by William Rysdyk and nicknamed "Rysdyk's Big Bull." He was Hambletonian, the ancestor of nearly every Standardbred now living. Hambletonian's sire was Abdullah, a Thoroughbred grandson of *Messenger, also an ugly-looking and ugly-acting animal. Abdullah was so despised, in fact, that his last owner got rid of him simply by turning him out on a barren beach to starve to death.

On his dam's side, Hambletonian was also rich in *Messenger blood, with many crossings of it. Many of the horses on his dam's side had "terrible tempers," too, but fortunately, his granddam (who was named One-Eye, having lost an eye in a tantrum-caused accident), was bred to gentle old Bellfounder, a famous Norfolk trotter, and Hambletonian inherited Bellfounder's sweet outlook on life.

One-Eye and Bellfounder produced "the Kent Mare," a good trotting racehorse and, later on, part of a fancy team of road mares until she was injured in a runaway. Then she was sold to Jonas Seely, who bought her for purely sentimental reasons—he had learned to ride on her granddam, Silvertail.

Seely's hired man, William Rysdyk, saw in this well-bred but crippled mare a chance to gain one of his fondest hopes. He wanted to own a good, money-making stallion. So he took the lame Kent Mare to his brother's place nearby where cantankerous, homely old Abdullah was then at stud, and the two were bred.

The result was all that Rysdyk had hoped for, a little bright bay stud colt. He loved the colt at first sight and immediately bought both him and the Kent Mare from Mr.

Seely for $125 (some of it "on time"). Not particularly interested in racing, Rysdyk put his bay colt to the stud at two years old. So good and so fast were his get that by the time he was only four years old, in 1853, he was a famous, sought-after sire, and his book that year boasted 101 mares.

Then the inevitable happened. People began to criticize Hambletonian, and the word got around that the reason Rysdyk never raced him was that he "couldn't trot." One man in particular, a Mr. Roe, who owned the stallion Abdullah Chief, got quite snide about this nonracing stud of Rysdyk's. This eventually angered Rysdyk, and in 1855 he had a handbill printed up and passed around New York:

In October next, I will trot my stallion Hambletonian against Seely C. Roe's Abdullah Chief over the Centerville Track, three races; one, two and three miles for $500 each in harness. As Mr. Roe has had so much to say about my not being willing to show the speed of my horse, I think he had better accept this challenge; and it may be that he will learn something about speed, and if he does not accept it, then I will bet him $5,000 that Hambletonian can trot one mile in less than 2.45.

Neither challenge was accepted, which must have been a huge disappointment after this buildup, but all talk of Hambletonian's not being able to trot ceased.

Before he died in 1876 he had sired over 1,300 foals, at least 150 of them superior breeding stallions, and had firmly established a new American breed, the Standardbred.

THE AMERICAN SADDLE HORSE

The year 1876 was notable in American horse history. It was the year during which Hambletonian died, grand old

Lexington died, and another new breed was officially born. In 1876, a "Breeders' Association" was formed, naming a Thoroughbred as "technical head of the American Saddle Horse breed."

That horse was Denmark. He was not imported, having been foaled in Kentucky in 1839. The American Saddle Horse, also known as the Saddlebred, is famous for its unequaled beauty, and it owes this beauty chiefly to its Thoroughbred ancestors, as well as much of its size, high style and brilliant, high-spirited temperament. Its famous "saddle gaits," however, it owes chiefly to those old Hobbie and Galloway descendants that very early paced and trotted and single-footed their way across this new country.

Long before Denmark was foaled, the American colonist and settler would not, by choice, ride anything but a "gaited horse." This attitude persisted long after the Hobbie lost favor in England.

As early as 1796, the Englishman had already forgotten his natural-gaited old favorite and was posting to the trot—to the point where he could visit the New World and write this incredible letter back home:

The horses in common use in Virginia are all of a light description, chiefly adapted for the saddle; some of them are handsome, but are for the most part spoiled by the false gaits which they are taught. The Virginians are wretched horsemen, as indeed are all the Americans I have met with, excepting some few in the neighborhood of New York. They ride with their toes just under the horse's nose, and their stirrup straps left extremely long, and the saddle being put three or four inches on the mane. As for the management of the reins, it is what they have no conception of. A trot is odious to them, and they express the utmost astonishment at a person who can like that uneasy gait, as they call it. The favorite gaits which all their horses are taught are a pace and a rack. In the first the animal moves his two feet on one side at the same time and gets on with a sort of shuffling motion, being unable to spring from the ground on these two feet, as in a trot. We should call this an unnatural gait, as none of their horses would ever move in that manner without a rider; but the Americans insist upon it that it is otherwise, because many of their colts pace as soon as born . . . But it is not one in five hundred that would pace without being taught.

No one, it seems, could convince this Englishman that what the Americans said was true. And as John Wallace pointed out, had he "known the history of the horses of his own country he would have known that from the time of King John to that of James I, the pacer was the most popular and fashionable horse in England." Then Mr. Wallace goes on in his typical, crusty manner:

The pacers our travelor saw in Virginia were the lineal descendants of the original English stock . . . and the awkward riding charged upon the Virginians, with some evident exaggerations, was wisely and sensibly adapted to the action of the horses they were riding. The criticism of the long stirrups is wholly unjust, as they are just the right length for the "military" seat, and nobody in this country when mounted on a *real saddle horse* would ever think of taking any other. The Englishman, when mounted on his "bonesetter," is compelled to have his stirrups short so that he can rise and fall with every revolution the horse makes on the trot to save himself from being shaken to death.

That was the situation in 1796. The Americans ignored the Englishman's scorn and went right on riding "real saddle horses" that didn't shake them to death and breeding ever better ones, culminating in the "realest" of them all, the American Saddle Horse. Besides pacing, which seems to today's riders a rough gait, those early ancestors of the Saddlebred could also single-foot. A single-foot is really any gait in which only one hoof strikes the ground at a time. It had, and has, many variations, known as the amble, the broken pace, the slow gait, the rack, etc., but they are all four-beat gaits, and most are almost indistinguishable from the others. They are all extremely "soft" and comfortable to ride, there being no up-and-down motion whatever, but only, at high speeds as in the rack (up to thirty miles an hour), a slight vibration.

Those early Hobbie descendants, then, were crossed with Thoroughbreds to get the American Saddle Horse, first known as the Kentucky Saddler. A quick glance at some old pedigrees shows innumerable Thoroughbred stallions involved, such as Denmark, *Messenger, Gray Eagle, Wagner, *Diomed, Sir Archy, and *Messenger's son, Mambrino. Much of this same native, saddle-gaited, and Thoroughbred cross went into another "branch," the Tennessee Walker. But since so much Morgan blood also went into both these new breeds, perhaps we'd better take a look at Justin Morgan's horse first.

THE MORGAN

No one would deny the Morgan breed its many fine qualities or its influence on newer breeds. There is a serious question, however, as to whether or not there was an appreciable amount of Thoroughbred blood in the original Morgan horse.

I don't know what the official story is on the Morgan right now, but for a long time there were many who claimed that the first Morgan was sired by a Thoroughbred that went by the two names of True Briton and Beautiful Bay. This may be true, but no authentic documents have been found to prove it. Whether Justin Morgan's horse was sired by a

Thoroughbred or not, it is certain that he had no noticeable Thoroughbred characteristics and that he carried a great deal of the old pacing-trotting native stock in him. Although the Morgan is claimed to be the first and oldest American breed, this would be difficult to prove because the origins of most other breeds are so nebulous.

Justin Morgan's horse was apparently foaled about 1789, and since he was indisputably the first Morgan, a prepotent mutation, the exact beginning of that breed is pretty clear-cut. But while Denmark was not foaled until 1839, the "saddle-gaited horse" as a distinct type had existed for centuries, so exactly when did the "saddle horse" originate? This is, of course, impossible to pinpoint.

In any case, the Morgans were supreme on the roads and trotting tracks of America for a short time, until the larger and faster Standardbreds took over. Meanwhile, along with the other foundation stock, the Morgans are also quite numerous in early Saddlebred and Walking Horse pedigrees, perhaps especially the Walkers.

THE TENNESSEE WALKING HORSE

The Tennessee Walker, or "Plantation Horse," is an excellent example of the way a new, distinctive breed can be evolved from many different breeds and strains. First, of course, there were the native pacers, trotters, and single-footers that were numerous in those days. The Thoroughbreds were there, too, many of them the same ones that contributed to the Kentucky Saddlers across the river.

One of them, McMeen's Traveler, a descendant of Boston and *Diomed, was a very famous pacer before the Civil War, as was "Allan," now the recognized primary foundation sire of the Walkers. One of Allan's ancestors was Black

Hawk, by Sherman Morgan, by Justin Morgan. Many other Morgans also figure in early Walker pedigrees. Even the Standardbreds got into the picture.

An extremely influential sire was Roan Allen, by Allan, who was black. Roan Allen appears in most Walker pedigrees today, and roan and black are still dominant colors in the breed. Roan Allen's granddam was "a Denmark mare," and Giovanni, a Saddlebred stallion, did much to add fineness or delicacy, which is more a Saddle Horse than a Walker trait.

And so, a virtual melting pot, the Tennessee Walker boasts the best blood of several fine breeds, yet has unique qualities all its own, the most noticeable being its "running walk," a gliding, overstriding gait that the Tennessee breeders developed from those early single-footers while the Kentucky breeders were developing the modern Saddlebred's slow gait and rack. Some like to think of the Walker as an early offshoot of the Saddle Horse, but it would probably be fairer to say that they were both offshoots of the common little saddle-gaited descendants of the Irish Hobbie. In any event, the Thoroughbreds contributed strongly to both new breeds, as they did to all these purely American breeds except the Morgan. The Thoroughbred influence can never be exaggerated, since it was in fact a prime force.

19

Eclipse to Secretariat

WHAT MIGHT be called "modern racing" really began around 1900. As early as 1905, a highly opinionated and rather blunt old gentleman named Thomas B. Merry complained about the then-new business of racing two-year-olds. He muttered:

As long as it takes but $10 to nominate a mare in the Futurity . . . just so long will extensive breeders . . . , who own from fifty to one hundred matrons, continue to nominate the produce of their mares in the Futurity; and as a natural consequence, from 200 to 500 good two-year-olds are annually knocked to pieces in a vain effort to bring them to the post in the great Futurity. . . . At the bottom of all this there can be nothing but greed. I speak plainly on matters of this sort, as I do on nearly everything else.

Well, you can't get much plainer! And as things have

turned out, Mr. Merry's opinion seems to be holding up. But it is no longer a simple matter of horse owners being greedy. It has become extremely expensive to get, raise, and race a good racehorse, starting with a stud fee that can easily be more than $5,000. It becomes a necessity for many to start a horse toward winning money as soon as possible.

The main greed has been that of the states in which races are held. The parimutuel system helped clean up and save racing, but it also made the states realize that here, in this huge amount of money being wagered through the parimutuel system, was a real gold mine of taxable income. And like all governments, the more money the states get, the more they want.

That's why the states encourage the racing of two-year-olds. More tracks are opened, and more racing days allotted to each track, to increase the gate and the wagering receipts. This means that since a horse can only run in so many races, more horses are needed to fill the cards. And when not enough mature horses are available, the two-year-olds are encouraged by more short-distance races for them. The horse owners, therefore, are not alone to blame.

It is still a fact, as it was in 1905, that hundreds—probably thousands now—of potentially good racehorses are broken down or burned up as two-year-olds. A two-year-old horse is still a baby in most respects. Its joints haven't even grown together yet. So they are often permanently lamed by this too-early, too-hard running. Although American breeders are turning out more and more foals each year, it has become almost a race to see if the supply can keep up with the growing demand and the annual loss of two-year-olds.

Still, enough colts and fillies have survived that third year of life to give us some good racehorses. And the purses have got so high that some of them have been millionaires.

Citation was our first millionaire, winning $1,085,760 in

forty-five races. He was a bay, owned by the famous Calumet Farm in Kentucky. Citation was also 1948's Triple Crown winner, the last one until 1973—a twenty-five-year gap.

Calumet has owned many outstanding horses: Whirlaway, another Triple Crown winner (1941); Pensive, almost a Triple Crown winner in 1944 (he lost the Belmont by half a length); Ponder, the horse famous for his heart-stopping come-up-from-*way*-behind finishes, who won the 1949 Derby in just that way; and three other Derby winners, Hill Gail (1952), Iron Liege (1957), and the courageous Tim Tam, who won both the Derby and the Preakness in 1958 and came in second in the Belmont on a fractured sesamoid bone.

Much of Calumet's success has been due to its great stallion Bull Lea. The sire of many of the horses mentioned above, Bull Lea's get in all have won about 2,000 first places, countless seconds and thirds, and more than $13 million in purses. This kindly, gentle stallion was helped by the fact that many of his "wives" were by another great stallion, *Blenheim II. Calumet's fine trainers, Ben and Jimmy Jones, were no small factor in the farm's success, either.

At Claiborne Farm, another prominent Kentucky establishment, *Nasrullah was at stud from 1950 to 1959, and from this Irish-bred stallion have come such racing giants as *Noor, Bold Ruler (the sire of 1973 Triple Crown winner, Secretariat), Nashua, and Roundtable, who won more than a million and became such a famous sire that a few years later his yearlings were selling for an average price of $43,900.

The Kentucky farm of the Texas-based King Ranch has also produced some great horses. One of its greatest, Bold Venture, was another horse that just missed winning the

Triple Crown. After winning the Derby and the Preakness, he was favored to win the Belmont but broke down before it was run. He got even, however, by siring Assault, who won the Triple Crown in 1946. Another son, Middleground, repeated Bold Venture's performance by winning only the first two of the big three.

Assault, Bold Venture's best son, had a peculiarity that worried some racegoers. When a year old, he'd hurt one forehoof, and though it was completely cured, he got into the habit of favoring it, walking and trotting oddly. But, as Silent Tom, Seabiscuit's trainer, might have said, "Runs, though."

King Ranch may unfortunately be best known for its one big mistake. It let a "good one" get away when it sold Stymie in a $1,500 claiming race. Stymie then went on to earn his new owner just a few dollars short of a million.

The list is endless, and nowhere near all the really good horses of the twentieth century can be mentioned here. Even the list of millionaires is a longish one: Citation, Carry Back, Nashua, Buckpasser, Roundtable, and the great gelding Kelso, who won close to *two* million.

The modern Thoroughbred comes as close as anything yet to the Duke of Cumberland's dream of a perfect racehorse. And this country registered about 25,000 new Thoroughbred foals in 1970, as compared, for instance, to only 5,819 in 1945. Because of this high standard of quality and the great numbers of Thoroughbreds, it has become much harder nowadays for a special one to stand out. That may partially explain why it took over fifty years for another horse to create anything near the sensation that Man o' War did in 1920 and twenty-five years since Citation for a Triple Crown winner. The horse that accomplished both these feats is a big chestnut stallion named Secretariat.

These words are being written the day after the 1973 Belmont Stakes, and for once the fan can be an eyewitness to all three Triple Crown races, thanks to television.

Secretariat came to the Derby in May a favorite, based on his two-year-old form. In 1972 he had already showed his style by becoming Horse of the Year as a mere two-year-old. But he was also the center of much controversy. Secretariat is a son of Bold Ruler, a great racehorse in his day but said to be incapable of siring horses that can go a distance. The Derby would be Secretariat's first test in a mile-and-a-quarter race, and his trainer, Lucien Laurin, was told repeatedly that Bold Ruler colts could not stand the distance. Secretariat's dam, Somethingroyal, however, was sired by Princequillo, a stallion famous for getting distance horses, and Mr. Laurin quietly trained his big colt and kept his own council. Meanwhile, all during Derby Week, the trainer of Sham, Secretariat's best rival, kept needling Mr. Laurin to bet $5,000 that Sham couldn't beat Secretariat. On top of this, rumors flew that Secretariat was not sound.

It was a rough week for trainer Laurin, but on Derby Day he was well rewarded by his horse's race. Not only did Secretariat win the Derby, proving both his soundness and his gameness, but he broke the track record by three-fifths of a second and astonished everyone by picking up speed steadily as he went, running each quarter-mile faster than the last—a pretty good indication that distance didn't bother him. He and his rider, Ron Turcotte, followed their accustomed pattern in the Derby, trailing until the final turn, then taking over and drawing away the rest of the race.

Two weeks later, in the mile-and-$\frac{3}{16}$ Preakness, Secretariat ran an even more spectacular race. It was hardly believable. First, there was that big red Secretariat, in his blue-and-white-checkered blinker hood, trailing the field.

Then suddenly there he was on the outside, passing horses as though they were trotting down a country lane! In seconds he had taken the lead. He held it without a touch of the whip, while Sham pushed him gallantly under punishment. It was too much for Sham, though, and Secretariat won the second jewel of the Triple Crown "going away." Unofficial clockers give him a record-setting time for this race, too, but he was not credited with it because the official timing device malfunctioned.

One leg of the Crown to go, the mile-and-a-half Belmont Stakes. The tension around Secretariat's stall grew nearly unbearable. Most trainers agree that it is harder to keep a big horse sound and fit than a small one, and Secretariat, at about 1,200 pounds, is a big one. He is also a glutton. A growing boy, he needed a lot of food—sixteen quarts of grain a day and a constant supply of hay—and that meant harder workouts between races to turn all those calories into muscle instead of fat. In Mr. Laurin's favor, though, was Secretariat's mild disposition. He took things in his 25-foot stride, and the constant interviewing, picture taking, and just plain gawking did not seem to fluster him a bit. Far from getting nervous and going off his feed, he stared right back at people and never overlooked an oat.

The Belmont Stakes, on June 9, 1973, was an historical event and a race to remember. On Secretariat's broad back rode the hopes of a nation. After twenty-five years, a Triple Crown winner seemed really possible at last. About 70,000 people were at Belmont Park, and millions more were glued to their television screens—all hoping.

Sham, who had done very well in the Derby and the Preakness, came out on the track first to no noticeable applause. Then Ron Turcotte rode Secretariat out, and the crowd went wild. Secretariat was the favorite in every respect.

And it was on this day that Secretariat won his right to the title "superhorse." He proved he could win at any distance and in any way he wanted.

There were five horses in the field, but after a few strides only two of them mattered. Far ahead of the other three, Secretariat and Sham held a short match race, head and head. Sham put up a gallant battle, but soon Secretariat's blistering speed burned the smaller horse out. Sham's head lifted slightly, and he began to fall back. From then on it was a one-horse race. Secretariat's long, seemingly effortless stride carried him farther and farther from all the rest, again without one touch of the whip. He was obviously running for the love of running. While the huge crowd screamed itself hoarse, Secretariat calmly and efficiently won the 105th Belmont Stakes by thirty-one lengths and broke the record by an incredible $2\frac{3}{5}$ seconds! Then he turned and ambled back, barely sweating, to claim his trophy, the immense Triple Crown trophy that had been waiting for him for twenty-five years.

The roses, the daisies, and now the carnations—and all won in a fashion that left no doubt in anyone's mind as to Secretariat's right to them. Regardless of what he does after this Triple Crown victory, Secretariat deserves to be added to the list of superhorses, horses that have won more than races, more than money, horses that have won the hearts of the people.

And Secretariat has done even more than that. He has revitalized the nation's interest in racing with his sensational accomplishments and his lovable personality. Perhaps most important of all, he has revitalized the spark of hope, that never-dying maybe in the heart of every Thoroughbred breeder in America. It took more than fifty years, but another superhorse did come along. And maybe—just maybe—that little red colt over there showing his heels to all the rest will be the next superhorse.

The Duke of Cumberland would have been very pleased with the modern American Thoroughbred.

Bibliography

Alexander, D. *The History and Romance of the Horse*. New York: Cooper Square Publishers, 1965.

———. *A Sound of Horses*. New York: Bobbs-Merrill, 1966.

Basler, R. P. *A Short History of the American Civil War*. New York: Basic Books, 1967.

Beckwith, B. K. *Step and Go Together*. Cranbury, N.J.: A. S. Barnes, 1967.

Boak, Slosson, and Anderson. *World History*. Boston: Houghton Mifflin, 1942.

Cooper, P. and Treat, R. L. *Man o' War*. New York: Julian Messner, 1950.

Gianoli, L., *et al. Horses and Horsemanship Through the Ages*. New York: Crown, 1969.

Howard, R. W. *The Horse in America*. Chicago: Follett, 1965.

Hunt, F. and Hunt, R. *Horses and Heroes*. New York: Scribner's, 1949.

Merry, T. B. *The American Thoroughbred*. Los Angeles: The Commercial Printing House, 1905.

Nagler, B. *The American Horse*. New York: Macmillan, 1966.

Newman, N. R. *Famous Horses of the American Turf*. New York: The Derrydale Press, 1932.

Osborne, W. D. *The Thoroughbred World.* Cleveland, Ohio: World, 1971.

Robertson, W. P. *The History of Thoroughbred Racing in America.* Englewood Cliffs, N.J.: Prentice-Hall, 1964.

Ross, J. K. M. *Boots and Saddles.* New York: Dutton, 1956.

Russell, G. B. *Hoofprints in Time.* Cranbury, N.J.: A. S. Barnes, 1966.

Scharf, E. E. *Famous Saddle Horses.* Louisville, Ky.: Standard Printing Co., 1936.

Stong, P. *Horses and Americans.* Garden City, N.Y.: Garden City Pub. Co., 1939, 1946.

Trevathan, C. E. *The American Thoroughbred.* New York: Macmillan, 1905.

Wallace, J. H. *The Horse of America.* New York: Published by the Author, 1897.